PENGUIN BOOKS

MOTORWORLD

Jeremy Clarkson made his name presenting a poky motoring
programme on BBC2 called *Top Gear*. He left to forge a career in
other directions but made a complete hash of everything and ended up
back on *Top Gear* again. He lives with his wife, Francie, and three
children in Oxfordshire. Despite this, he has a clean driving licence.

Motorworld

JEREMY CLARKSON

PENGUIN BOOKS

For Francie

PENGUIN BOOKS

Published by the Penguin Group
Penguin Books Ltd, 80 Strand, London WC2R ORL, England
Penguin Group (USA) Inc., 375 Hudson Street, New York, New York 10014, USA
Penguin Books Australia Ltd, 250 Camberwell Road, Camberwell, Victoria 3124, Australia
Penguin Books Canada Ltd, 10 Alcorn Avenue, Toronto, Ontario, Canada M4V 3B2
Penguin Books India (P) Ltd, 11 Community Centre, Panchsheel Park, New Delhi – 110 017, India
Penguin Group (NZ), cnr Airborne and Rosedale Roads, Albany, Auckland 1310, New Zealand
Penguin Books (South Africa) (Pty) Ltd, 24 Sturdee Avenue, Rosebank 2196, South Africa

Penguin Books Ltd, Registered Offices: 80 Strand, London WC2R ORL, England

www.penguin.com

First published by BBC Books (to accompany the BBC television series) 1996
This edition published in Penguin Books 2004
23

Copyright © Jeremy Clarkson, 1996, 2004
All rights reserved

The moral right of the author has been asserted

Set by Rowland Phototypesetting Ltd, Bury St Edmunds, Suffolk
Printed in England by Clays Ltd, St Ives plc

Except in the United States of America, this book is sold subject
to the condition that it shall not, by way of trade or otherwise, be lent,
re-sold, hired out, or otherwise circulated without the publisher's
prior consent in any form of binding or cover other than that in
which it is published and without a similar condition including this
condition being imposed on the subsequent purchaser

ISBN-13: 978-0-141-01787-7

Contents

Extreme Machines

Italy

I've been fortunate enough over the years to stay in many truly outstanding hotels where obsequious waiters compete for your attention with the view – hard when it's Hong Kong harbour, San Francisco Bay or St Mark's. But my favourite is the Locanda del Sant' Uffizio-Da Beppé in Asti, where I stayed when we were filming the Fiat Coupé for *Top Gear*.

It's a beautiful building, the food is as good as you'll eat anywhere and the owner redefines the concept of friendliness. Here's a man who would very probably stick his tongue down your throat if you ever went back for second helpings.

But I enjoyed my four-day stay there most of all because over lunch, on the second day, we shared the dining room with an Italian family.

I'm not talking here about a bearded father in grey shoes, a woman called Janet in Marks and Spencer's finest and two children. I'm not talking about the near-silence that accompanies most British family days out.

No, here we had granddad and grandma, her mother, their six children, various in-laws and an indeterminate number of grandchildren. It was impossible to say how many exactly because they were never all at the table at the same time – they'd get one seated and another would be off, making tyre-squealing noises round the dessert trolley.

It was a huge feast which appeared to have been ruined as the eighth course was being cleared. Two of the sons started to argue so loudly that pretty quickly everyone within twelve feet was sucked in. Minutes later, it was out of control.

Arms and legs were flailing from one side of the room to the other. Granny was on her feet, pointing at one of her daughters, who looked fit to burst. The babies were screaming. This was one big family bust-up.

Which turned out to be about the Fiat Tipo – or, specifically, how economical it is. In Italy, a family hatch-back can tear apart a family.

Now, if they get this passionate over the Fiat Tipo, can you begin to imagine what it's like to drive there? Well, I'll tell you. Like a roller-coaster without rules.

The road from Turin down to the Italian Riviera is one of the most beautiful in Europe, but on this occasion it was being ruined.

It wasn't that the ancient Fiat Ritmo in front was being driven slowly – far from it – but I had a 3.0-litre V6 Alfa Romeo and I wanted to go even faster. I wanted to hear that magnificent engine sing because stuck behind that Fiat it was only humming.

Eventually, the road straightened out and, as I passed, I noticed that the driver of the Fiat was a toothless peasant farmer who'd seen at least 80 summers. His face was as wizened as a walnut and about the same colour too. It could well have been a walnut, actually.

But then I got down to the job in hand – having fun with a great car, on a great road, in a great country – and Walnut Face was erased from the memory.

This was a mistake because, fifteen miles later, he was back. I'd pulled onto the wrong side of the road to make the oncoming hairpin less tight and he shot through on the inside, wheels locked and grinning the grin of a madman. He really was as nutty as he looked.

For fifteen miles I'd strained to read the road ahead, not realising that the real danger was darting about in my rearview mirror. Walnut Face had been overtaken and he was going to get back in the lead if it bloody killed him. Welcome to Italy, where all the world, it seems, is a racetrack.

You want proof. Okay, here it comes. Two years later, I was flat out on the autostrada but this wasn't good enough for the car behind which desperately, and very obviously, wanted to get past. It was close enough for me to notice, through the glare of its headlights, that it contained four nuns.

Shortly afterwards I was testing a Sierra Cosworth in Sicily and wanted to see if Ford's claimed top speed of 150 mph was accurate. The road was straight and so I went for it.

But as I was eking out the last vestiges of power, doing about 147 mph, I encountered a police van trundling along the inside lane which caused me to brake, shall we say, pretty violently. The door of the van slid back and out came a uniformed arm.

This was big trouble . . . except for one small thing. This was Italy, and the hand was ordering me to go faster. These guys also wanted to know how fast a Sierra Cosworth would go so they could discuss it, noisily and with much fork pointing, over supper that night.

As Professor Franco Ferrarotti of Rome University put it, 'We have a speed limit in Italy, of course. It is the top speed of your car.'

Giovanni Agnelli, the most powerful man in the country and the owner of Fiat, among other things, goes further. 'Let's say the Italians are very hard to discipline, especially if it's something they don't like.'

If someone introduces a law there which doesn't go down well with the people, they don't organise protest marches, they just ignore it. And because the police are people too, they don't bother trying to enforce it either.

Speeding is a big thing. Only very recently, a social democratic minister made a big stand on the issue, getting on one or other of the country's 1200 television stations every night to talk about the dangers of driving too quickly. He imposed new laws, whipped up the police and was rewarded with the sack.

In Italy, you sometimes get the impression they'd be happier to lose the Pope than to lose their right to drive like maniacs.

The question that immediately springs to mind at this point is, why? I mean, we're talking here about a country that thinks an emergency plumber is someone who can get to you within seven weeks.

That's six weeks to process the order, six days to order the parts and 23 hours and 59 minutes arguing with the suppliers.

The actual drive from his workshop to your house, 19 miles away, is done in 30 seconds. Now, why should this be so? Why should Italians be so much faster and wilder on the roads than, say, the Germans or the British or the Spanish?

Experts point to the fact that Italy has been governed over the centuries by a myriad of different rulers. Just when the people got used to one set of ideas and one set of rules, another guy would come along and change everything. Remember, Italy has had 50 governments since the war.

So, individualism is a big thing. In Italy, the most important thing is to enjoy life, and if that means a few rules are broken, so what? The rules will change pretty soon anyway. The foot, they say, is more important than the shoe.

On top of this, Italy has only been a consumerist, industrialised country for one generation and they still can't really believe that they can actually go down to the town and buy a car.

There was never a lengthy period when only the rich drove cars, giving them the cachet they've earned elsewhere in the world. One minute there were no cars and then bang, all of a sudden everyone had a replacement for their horse or bicycle.

The car in Italy has no appeal as a status symbol, says Professor Ferrarotti. 'Italians love the way they are made. They have a fascination with machinery and driving a car blends in with our anarchistic bent.

'You know it's not difficult to govern the Italians – just

unnecessary. You can have all sorts of laws here, just so long as they're not enforced.'

And you only need to look around Rome to see what he means. The law says everyone has to wear a seat belt. But no one does.

The professor thinks he has a reason for this. 'Of course, seat belts are very important and the Italians are the first ones to admit it . . . theoretically. But if you had to use your damn seat belt every time you got into your little Punto or your big Ferrari – if there are any such things in a Ferrari – well, it is like betting against yourself. It might invite disaster.

'Italians are very superstitious and if you wear a seat belt it displays a lack of confidence in yourself. Seat belts are a real threat to public safety. They should be abolished.

'If you put your seat belt on before you even start the engine, that means you are, at a minimum, a mediocre driver. You should not be behind the wheel. Your permit should be taken away.'

So here we have a country where people don't obey rules that aren't really enforced anyway, a country that is in love with machinery and, most of all, a country that was only recently introduced to the car. The love is still strong.

Elsewhere in the industrialised world, except Switzerland, the first flush of the relationship has gone, the mistress has become a wife and everyone's more interested in its ability to cook, to sew and to be safe. I know my Mercedes is fat but she makes great hollandaise sauce. In Italy, on the other hand, they don't give a damn if the windscreen wipers foul the steering wheel so long as it looks good. They want the car to be a pouting teenager, to be great in bed and with legs that go on for 26 miles.

They may drive a Fiat Punto but what they want is a Ferrari Testarossa. And until they get one, they will pretend the Punto has a 5.0-litre V12 with red camshaft covers.

In the world there are five serious supercar manufacturers and it should be no surprise to find that three are based in Italy – Ferrari, Lamborghini and Bugatti. What is odd is that they're all made within fifteen miles of one town – Modena.

I've been there and it's an ordinary, communist-run, peasanty sort of place which you might even call a bit shabby. The people have that Mediterranean look about them – ill-fitting suit trousers, belts fashioned from bailer twine, bad hats and even worse teeth. They sit around in medieval squares, chatting and smoking, only looking up to stare at a car. And there's the difference.

I asked Giovanni Agnelli what makes the people of Modena tick and he said, 'They have a mania for mechanics there. When a motorbike goes by, they can tell you what sort of engine it has. Ferrari is there. There's a tractor factory there . . .'

A cruel one that, because Lamborghini started out as a tractor manufacturer and remains one of just two Italian car firms that Mr Agnelli doesn't own. He already has Fiat, Ferrari, Lancia, Alfa Romeo, Maserati and Piaggio. But then he also controls around 25 per cent of all companies quoted on the Italian stock exchange, Juventus football club, the newspaper *La Stampa*, Sestriere ski resort and a few small concerns outside Italy – like NASA.

On official business, Snr Agnelli has a Fiat Croma – a bicycle – but for pleasure I happen to know he has a Ferrari 456.

That makes him pretty special in Italy. When you drive a car like that over there, you are revered as a sort of cross between the Virgin Mary, Gilles Villeneuve and Roberto Baggio.

When we were over there making the BBC series *Motorworld* we drove through a selection of hilltop villages with quite a convoy. Up front, I led the way in a Ferrari 355. Behind was the director in his Bugatti EB110 and bringing up the rear was the producer in a piece of purple haze, a dollop of rolling thunder they call the Lamborghini Diablo.

To see one of these cars in a lifetime is a special thing, but to find all three in a village is like coming home from work to find Halley's Comet sitting by the fire. The Ferrari brought people out of their houses, the Bugatti got them cheering and the Lamborghini caused more than a few to faint.

In England, if you took a convoy like that through a village, the parish councillors would storm off down to the scout hut where plans would be drawn up for a bypass and 6-foot-high speed bumps on the High Street.

But I shall take to my grave the sight of a small boy in Italy. He couldn't have been more than six and he was beside himself with excitement – he didn't know whether to point or to tug at his mother's dress and, if he did point, which car should he point at?

We stopped there for a drink and the town just ground to a halt. They came out of the school, out of the shops and out of their houses and they wanted to see the engines, the interiors, the suspension. And when we left, they wanted to see six black lines right down the main street.

Sadly though, because the Bugatti had four-wheel drive, they only got four.

That said, the Bugatti had disappeared from view first. It's an interesting car this; mainly because someone, some-where, sat down and said, 'I know. Let's give it twelve cylinders, sixty valves, four camshafts and two turbo-chargers.' And then someone else must have said, 'No, let's not be homosexual about this. Let's give it four turbos.'

It's the fastest Italian car but it's not the loudest – that accolade rests with the Diablo, which really is a 5.7-litre vibrator, a truck and a chest of drawers with a rocket motor. If you want a wild ride, this is where you queue.

But if you want the best car in the world, you must have the Ferrari, which is by far and away the nicest car I will ever drive. I love the way it looks, I love its engine and I love, most of all, everything it stands for. Ferrari, in my book, is a pagan god, a steel deity, sex on wheels. And that 355 represents automotive perfection.

Ordinarily, when the rear end of a car starts to slide, I undo my seat belt and get in the back, but in the 355, you just dial in a touch of opposite lock and then marvel as the car simply sorts itself out.

In an instant, you're back on the power, willing that 40-valve, 3.5-litre V8 onwards, slamming the gear lever through its chromed gate and glancing occasionally at the simple white-on-black rev counter. This car has the delicacy of a quail's egg dipped in celery salt and the power of a chicken chilli jalfrezi.

But that's only half the story. I could derive as much pleasure from putting this car in my sitting room and just looking at it as I could from driving it every day. And never mind that it sounds better than Puccini and can outrun a Tornado jet.

That's not it.

This is a car that was made by people who love cars, and it shows.

They don't love cars in Germany or Japan or even America. Car manufacturers there strive to get each of the component parts right, to make the product fulfil the dictionary definition of a car as closely as is possible. But passion is not part of the equation.

You could probably drive a big BMW round a racetrack faster than a Ferrari 355 and the BMW engineers would be pleased. 'Our car is faster than their car,' they would say as they put on their checked jackets and stroked their pointy beards.

They would be so busy congratulating themselves that they'd miss the point. The man in the Bee Em will feel like he's just had a bath, and the man in the Ferrari will feel like he's just had sex with Claudia Schiffer and Elle Macpherson. At the same time.

That's because a Ferrari has soul and a BMW does not. A BMW is an engineering masterpiece but a Ferrari is so much more than that.

Look at the fuel filler cap. It's not simply a device to keep your petrol in the tank. It's actually been styled. Then there's the gear lever. It's a work of art. Every component in a Ferrari has to do more than simply fulfil its function.

And it isn't just Ferrari, either. Look at the 3-litre Alfa Romeo engine. This is fitted to their equivalent of a Ford Mondeo. If it weren't for some pretty stupid taxation laws over there, this is the engine that would power Mr Fertiliser Salesman to his next meeting.

Now, elsewhere in the world, an engine is simply a collection of bits, nailed rather inelegantly together. I love cars but engines bore me even more than double chemistry did on a Saturday morning. Engines are simply there to make cars move. The end.

Er . . . not quite. I haven't a clue what makes the Alfa V6 different but here is a power unit that's pure opera. While every motor in the world sounds like someone singing in the bath, this is the full Pavarotti.

When the rev counter climbs past 5500 rpm, conversation in the cockpit just stops. People who would rather have their legs amputated than talk about cars will actually ask what on earth is under the bonnet – the London Symphony Orchestra or the Berlin Philharmonic? One girl asked me to stop revving the engine so high because she kept sticking to the seat.

Then there's the styling. At the end of the eighties, all cars were beginning to look not just similar but absolutely identical. Car companies were employing designers from all over the world in their styling centres and national identity was going out of the window. The same set of parameters were being fed into the same computers all over the world and the same answers were coming back.

And the investment became so high that car companies began to counsel ordinary people for their opinions. If you're going to spend a billion dollars on a new car, you want to make absolutely sure it will sell, so you drag people off the street and show them the various design options.

And, ten times out of ten, these dreadful people in their cardigans and their sandals will opt for the least imaginative.

Italy saved the day, first of all with the Punto which, initially, looked like something from Iceland, it was so radical. But now, a few years down the line, we can see it for what it is: a truly neat piece of design. And then there was the Fiat Coupé and, more recently, the wonderfully wild Alfa Romeo 145.

Cars like these have put Italian styling houses back on the map, which is a good thing because no one can create a car quite like them.

This is perhaps because Italy has a monopoly on style. I don't care how many times Jeff Banks tells me that this year, London or New York, or even Paris, has taken over the mantle and become fashion torchbearer, I *know* the world fashion capital is Milan.

In England on a hot day, women are happy to walk around with their bra straps showing. In Paris, they don't shave their armpits. And you just can't mention Germany and style in the same book, let alone the same sentence.

It's the same story in America, too, where the Farrah Fawcett hairdo of 1975 still reigns supreme.

In Italy, even the policemenists look like they've just come off a catwalk. One I found, standing on a rostrum in the middle of a Roman square, was immaculate, as was his routine. Each wave of the hand, each toot of the whistle and each twist of the body was Pans People perfect. Never mind that the traffic was completely ignoring him, he looked good, and that's what mattered. Looking good in Italy is even more important than looking where you're going.

Which is why I made a special effort to ensure my linen jacket was especially crumpled on my visit to Turin. The supercars may hail from Modena, and Alfa is up in Milan but, historically, Italy's coach-builders clustered around the big boy – Fiat – Fabbrica Italiana di Automobili Torino.

And as they sat there, waiting for Agnelli to commission this or that, or maybe a customer to want something a little different, they were surrounded by the best art in the world. Show me someone who says there are more beautiful buildings than those in Italy, or more beautiful art, or clothes, and I'll show you someone who's never been there.

When you're surrounded by such magnificence, it's bound to rub off. And that's why, when a car manufacturer wants something really special, he picks up the phone and calls one of three men: Giorgio Guigaro, Sergio Pininfarina or Nuccio Bertone.

Let me list a few of their past credits so you get the picture. The Mark One VW Golf and its coupé sister, the Scirocco. The Lexus Coupé. Every single Ferrari.

The Isuzu Piazza. The Peugeot 205. The Peugeot 504 convertible. The Alfa 164. The Peugeot 605. All the recent Maseratis, the Fiat Coupé, the Opel Manta . . . how long have you got?

And on top of this, the chaps roll up at various motor shows from time to time with 'concept cars' which then influence all the world's other designers. It is not unreasonable to say that 80 per cent of all cars on the road in the world today were designed in, or influenced by, Turin.

Turin is to car design what Melton Mowbray is to pork pies. I put this to Mr Guigaro. He said, 'Er . . . I think Turin is to cars what Silicon Valley is to computers.'

I didn't catch what Mr Pininfarina said because you don't listen when you're in the presence of greatness, and believe me he is great. He designed the 355. That makes him God in my eyes.

And there's a priest in Maranello who might agree with this. Don Erio Belloi is the spiritual leader in the village where Ferraris are made and where the race team is based.

On a Sunday, when the scarlet cars are out doing battle somewhere, this place is like a scene from *The Omega Man*, only Charlton Heston is at home watching the Grand Prix as well.

I wanted to interview Erio badly about the town's obsession with Ferrari, because I thought he'd moan a little bit about how the Formula One calendar clashed with his services.

The first indication that this might not be the exact tack of the interview came when he said we could meet at any time on Sunday except when the Grand Prix was on. And the second came when I was shown into his study. Instead of bibles, the bookshelves were groaning under the weight of Ferrari memorabilia, and the walls were plastered with technical drawings of the 456, pictures of Enzo – to whom he administered the last rites – and Gilles Villeneuve, his favourite driver.

Did he, I asked when the race finished, ever think unsaintly thoughts about other teams in the Grand Prix circus. 'Yes,' he replied a bit too quickly. 'It is bad to think if someone else dies [Ferrari] will win, but there is a bit of that.'

That's what you're dealing with in Italy when it comes to Ferrari. They don't have a Queen or a Princess Diana. They don't have cricket. They haven't had an empire for 2500 years. But they don't care because they've got Ferrari.

Here is the only team to have won Le Mans and the Formula One World Championship in the same year. And not just once either, but three times. Here is the only team in the world that makes its own engines and its own chassis. Here is the team which has won more Grand Prix than anyone else.

Italy has always been at the top of the sport, even before Ferrari came along in 1947. There was Maserati and, right up to the late fifties, Alfa Romeo too. In one year, Alfa were so dominant that their driver pulled into the pits on the last lap to get his car polished. Then it would look smart as it crossed the line.

If Michael Shoemaker did that today, Murray Walker would have a duck fit.

But do you know where all these old racing cars have

ended up? Well it certainly isn't Italy. If you want to find the best racing Alfas of yesteryear or the great GT Ferraris from the sixties, look in Switzerland or Britain or Japan.

This is because they became so valuable no one would ever dare to take them out on the road. Largely, they sit in hermetically sealed museums, roped off and assaulted with air conditioning. Many will never turn a wheel again.

And that, to an Italian, is just incomprehensible.

Cuba

The Caribbean: an arc of diamonds in a jewel-encrusted sea. Palm trees. Ice-white beaches. White-hot sun. And the gentle strains of Bob Marley to accompany your multi-coloured, multi-cultural early-evening drink. From Trinidad in the south to Cancún in the north, it's pretty much the same story, only the authors are different. Some of the islands were shaped by the British, some by the Dutch and others by the Spanish and French.

But then there's Cuba, whose most recent history was penned by Lenin. The colonial gloss is gone, or lost in the smoke from burning civilian planes which the Cuban air force has just shot down. Cuba could be one of the world's most sought-after holiday destinations. But thanks to Castro, it's beaten into 184th place by Filey.

Let me explain by reviewing a restaurant in Havana. Called *The 1830*, it's an elegant seafront property where a maître d' from 1955 bows an effusive welcome and clicks his fingers, indicating that a hitherto unseen minion should park your car.

Another click and another bowing minion, starched tea towel draped over his left arm, ushers you into one of the four dining rooms, each of which offers a fine view of the Gulf of Mexico.

The tablecloths are white linen and the glassware is

heavily leaded crystal. In 1955, this would have been one of the country's top eateries where you would have rubbed shoulders with Ernest Hemingway and Frank Sinatra.

Today, it is still one of the city's finest eateries but that's like saying the Mahindra Jeep is one of India's finest cars.

The first indication that all was not well came when we examined the fixtures and fittings more closely. The wood in the door frames was held together with worms and everything looked as though it had last seen a lick of paint in 1958. Which is probably about right. It turned out too that the glass was not leaded. It was heavy because of all the dirt on it.

Then there were the menus which talked of wild and exotic dishes, but none seemed to be available which is why I asked for spaghetti bolognese to start, followed by chicken and fresh vegetables.

Fifteen minutes passed, followed by a further fifteen minutes. Then, we waited a quarter of an hour while fifteen minutes slid by and then, all of a sudden, we noticed another fifteen minutes had gone by. Fifteen minutes afterwards, one of the white uniformed waiters wheeled some food to our table on his trolley.

There was my spaghetti bolognese and there too, surprisingly, were my vegetables, which looked as though they'd been put in the pan back when I'd applied for my visa. 'No,' I said, 'I want these vegetables with my chicken.' 'Certainly sir,' said the waiter. Actually, he spoke no English so it could have been, 'You miserable capitalist pig. I hope your wallet catches fire, fatty,' but never mind.

I knew the spaghetti was wrong just by looking at it.

There was a crust on the sauce which indicated, correctly, that it was stone cold. Again the smiling waiter arrived who, when he understood what I was on about, plunged his finger into the bolognese and nodded. Yes indeed, sir. It is cold.

Back it went and another fifteen minutes went by as they heated it up. There are no microwaves in Cuba. When it returned, the grated cheese had melted and merged with the pasta, which had been under a grill for a quarter of an hour. But none of this mattered because there, in the sauce, was the dimple mark where the waiter's finger had been for a wiggle.

I simply shoved it away and sat back to enjoy the sounds of Mrs Mills on the piano. She was terrible and her instrument was worse but I forgot about it when the French windows imploded. The disco outside had begun to pump 'Thriller' out at 400,000 decibels but Mrs Mills was unmoved; she soldiered on with her rendition of some fifties' favourite, proving what I'd begun to suspect. She was as deaf as one of the legs on her piano.

Then I noticed the smiling waiter bearing down once again with his trolley and my plate of vegetables which, after another half hour in the pan, had begun to resemble soup, and my chicken. Or was it?

To try to ensure they got a Michelin star, these people had obviously used one of the tyre company's products in their cuisine and now I was charged with the task of eating it. It was impossible so, again, I gave up and reached for my drink.

Which had gone. So keen were the staff to act like

top-quality hosts and hostesses, they tended to clear your glass the instant you put it down, whether it was empty or not. According to the bill, I'd had eighteen daiquiris, whereas my head the following morning suggested I'd had none.

The bill was £25 each, which explained why we were the only customers that night. Twenty-five pounds is what the average Cuban earns in five months. Cuba is, not to put too fine a point on it, fucked.

Since Russia went all lovey-dovey in 1991, aid to their former friend in the Caribbean has virtually dried up, which means petrol has soared to £2.50 a gallon and there are no takers for Castro's nickel, or his cigars or even his sugar. Iberia is the only major airline that flies from Europe to Havana, so you need to be a determined and persistent tourist to actually get there.

Then you have to find somewhere to stay. Cubans are banned from even the lobbies of the big hotels so the government feels free to charge what it likes for the rooms. And what it likes tends not to be what you and I like. They cost a bleeding fortune and all the services, being Russian, broke down four years ago and can't be fixed because there are no spare parts.

Against this sort of background, you would expect to find car-free streets but that simply isn't the case. They are chock-full of, mostly, American cars from the forties and fifties.

Even though America has had a trade embargo with Cuba for 30 years, ingenuity has kept these dinosaurs going . . . after a fashion.

I mean, let's face it: if, all of a sudden, no new cars were imported into Britain, you wouldn't throw your Cavalier away just because one of the windscreen wipers had come off. And even if there were no Halfords on every street corner you still wouldn't give up.

You'd jury-rig some kind of device to clear the windscreen when it rains, and that's what they've done in Cuba.

And they've gone further too. You couldn't possibly afford a can of brake fluid out there, even if you could find any, so they've worked out that a mixture of alcohol, sugar and shampoo does the job nearly as well.

But what about the engine? Surely, if that goes bang and you can't get parts, you really have had it? Nope. You simply remove the power unit from a Lada – and they were everywhere when the Russians were in town – and fit that instead.

Most of the old cars out there have Lada engines these days, which is a little sad. We met one chap with an Aston Martin DB4, and he really believed that one day, when Castro is gone, it will fetch $100,000. Well, apart from the complete lack of paint, the total absence of any interior trim and the Lada engine coupled with a Moscovitch gearbox, he might be right.

You see gullwing Mercedes-Benz, Chevvy Impalas, Cadillac Coupe de Villes and countless other rare breeds spluttering around on Lada power. And on every street corner, someone is hooking up a bucket of water to the mains power supply to recharge their 40-year-old battery.

God knows how this works but the sparks and the steam suggest some kind of reaction happens in the bucket. Some kind of reaction happens at the power station, too, which, in rural Cuba, only supplies power for four hours a day.

Obviously, any form of motorsport is right out of the question here, and not only because Che Guevara thought it was decadent. However, at weekends a few intrepid souls take their Lada-powered yank tanks to the old motorway out of Havana and race from bridge to bridge.

This is not high-speed stuff. Indeed, most of them – particularly one car, which started on petrol but switched over to cheaper kerosene when the engine was hot – couldn't even keep up with our Daihatsu tracking car.

They also have sumo events where two cars go head to head and try to push each other over a line painted in chalk on the road. Exciting it's not.

Finding Che Guevara's car, on the other hand, was. For twelve years it had been sitting in a garage, untouched and unloved, so that when we rolled into town no one even knew what sort of Chevrolet it was. And I know more about antique clocks than sixties' Americana so I can't enlighten you either, other than to say that it was knackered.

Nothing worked. Because it was a 'symbol of the revolution' no one had been allowed to swap the V8 for a Lada unit or replace the fifties' brake fluid with Wash 'n' Go.

We employed nine people at 50p a day each and set them to work on getting it going again while we went off to have some fun.

I have become a keen diver in recent years and had cunningly written a piece in the script which required me to appear under the water with a tank strapped to my back, preferably by a reef near a deserted white beach.

A small island off the south coast of Cuba was located, scouted and deemed to be perfect. They even had scuba gear there.

And it came with the personal recommendation of two Dutch guys who were out there buying up seafront properties. 'Oh yeah,' they said. 'It's a great little island but you've got to get there first . . .' And with that, they were gone, laughing strangely.

The next morning we found out why. The aeroplane was a small twin-engined thing which, from a distance, looked like a farmyard animal. Closer inspection revealed that the brownness was a result of much rust.

The tyres were flat and the engines were of a type that simply defied belief. If Karl Benz had come up with this version of internal combustion in the 1880s, he'd have given up and become a greengrocer.

Inside, things became worse. Much worse. There were no windows and the seats were only half-fastened to the floor. Seat belts? Forget it.

Miraculously, the engines fired and somehow the plane became airborne, I assume. Without windows it was hard to be sure but after five minutes I figured we would have hit something had we still been on the ground so I knew all was well.

Then it wasn't well at all because the entire cabin filled with smoke. No kidding, I had to endure a half-hour flight, not even being able to see that there were no windows. All I could see was those two Dutch guys laughing.

But then we were down in what looked like paradise.

Unusual birds sang strange songs in vivid trees. The water was aquamarine and the beaches really were as white as driven cocaine.

A gaily coloured bus which looked like it might have been used by Stalin himself took us to the hotel, which sat right on the beach. Perfect. Er . . . no.

Fashioned from concrete, it had water spurting from every air-conditioning unit but, surprisingly, the pool was empty. Good job too because in the scum which clung to the sides and floor I found life-forms that are in no books. David Attenborough could have made an entire series in it.

Most of the guests were on the beach, where we found the bar, a straw edifice which oozed charm and tranquillity. But the reason why it was so peaceful was simple. It had no drink. No beer. No rum. No Coke. Nothing.

And it was pretty much the same story in the dining room, though at least here there were some forlorn European honeymooners to laugh at as they picked their way through some rock-hard boiled eggs.

You just know what had gone on in the poor bloke's mind, before deciding to reject the Maldives and Mauritius and Antigua. I'll take her somewhere exotic, somewhere none of her friends have been. She'll be impressed. We'll go to Cuba.

Poor sods.

They couldn't even dive because we'd commandeered the only boat and the only two sets of scuba kit. And then the real fun and games began.

Keith, the cameraman, has the buoyancy of balsawood

and even when he wore a weight-belt that would have sunk a killer whale he was still having trouble getting below the surface, especially as he was burdened with an underwater camera which floated.

I had problems of my own though. My buoyancy vest leaked like a sieve so that it was a jet-propulsion pack. The torrent of escaping air rushed me around the reef like Marine Boy and frightened away all the fish too.

It was a pathetic spectacle. The world's most revered broadcasting organisation and we had a cameraman who wouldn't sink, a presenter who was doing Mach 2 and a director who couldn't dive and was forced to hang around on the surface with a snorkel.

Then our chartered captain had a heart attack. Probably from laughing at us.

It took two days to film our opening sequence for the programme, then it was time for THAT flight back. We were nervous without any real need because we had a different plane, which had windows.

And not much else. It had been built in Russia shortly after the war and last serviced in 1953. You would not believe how much smoke poured out of the engines as we trundled down the runway, dodging dogs, and lumbered into the air.

But as we settled down, I appreciated the view, which really was exquisite. It was a perfect summer's day, which meant one thing . . . thunderstorms.

I have been prone to exaggeration in the past but ask anyone on that plane what it was like and they'll start to quiver. It was truly the most terrifying half hour of my life as the plane bucked, writhed, turned upside down and plummeted.

I was forever being lifted from my seat, a worrying thing because I knew that just inches above my hair was a paddle fan. Would I be decapitated before we hit the deck? It seemed important.

I really did think we were going to die, but somehow I managed a smile because I thought of my daughter, who was one at the time, growing up knowing her daddy had died in a Russian plane, over Cuba, in a thunderstorm. It's a pretty cool way to go, let's face it.

We came out of the clouds at tree-top height and cruised at that level all the way to Havana with the lightning turning the wings blue every few seconds. And then we were back.

And in need of a drink, which meant heading for the Cohiba nightclub. It is assumed that researchers on a television programme only have to find the stories, but that's just part of it. They also have to find the best hotels and the best bars, and in Cuba Andy had excelled himself.

Not only did he have an endless supply of stories that went beyond the realms of 'amazing' but also he knew where to take us after a near-death experience at 30 feet.

Outside the Cohiba every night of the week hundreds and hundreds of girls hang around.

'Ah,' I said. 'Here are some more people waiting for the lift marshals to stop government-registered cars, so that they may get a lift home.'

'Er no,' replied Andy. 'It's not really like that here.'

Puzzled, I stepped out from our Daihatsu Sportrak and

was, within ten seconds, surrounded by a dozen or more pubescent girls who, for the most part, were wearing dental floss.

My word, I thought, these Sportraks have some serious pulling power, but I was a trifle wide of the mark. It seems that they were only interested in my wallet which would enable them to get into the hottest night-spot in town.

In return for the $10 entrance fee, I would have them as my escorts, at my beck and call, all week. Jesus.

Even more amazingly, one chap turned up in a Lamborghini Diablo, which seemed like overkill. You can get your leg over if you have ten bucks, leave alone a £150,000 automobile.

I was even on the receiving end of some smouldering come-ons when I tooled by on a bicycle which was powered by the motor from a fumigation pump. It wasn't the bike. It wasn't my good looks or flowing locks. It was my Visa card they wanted; that and a passport out of the place.

Technically, the girls aren't prostitutes in the accepted sense. In fact, they'll go further for less, which proves really how screwed-up the Caribbean's largest land-mass has become.

I found myself wondering, as I strolled round the museum dedicated to the revolution, if Castro and Guevara could possibly have foreseen that one day their people would be asked, by their government, to eat grass.

In fact, the museum is a hopeless waste of money in a country that doesn't have any. Inside a large glass tomb, there's the boat that brought the rebels over to Cuba, and outside, there are other mechanised pieces which have been preserved for all time.

There's Castro's Land Rover and a Supermarine fighter. Britain, it seems, has a lot to answer for. There's also a bulldozer which had been converted into a tank, and various vans which had been used to storm the palace and so on.

But, frankly, none of this matters alongside Arnol Rodríguez, who is a living, breathing relic from those revolutionary days.

Along with eight other commandos, on the eve of the 1958 Cuban Grand Prix, he kidnapped Juan Manuel Fangio, who, at the time, was like Michael Schumacher, Alain Prost and Ayrton Senna all rolled into one.

At gunpoint they bundled him out of the Hotel Lincoln, into one of three waiting cars and took him across town to a rather ordinary two-storey house. Inside were a mother and two daughters, revolutionaries to the core, who led him upstairs and gave him steak and salad.

The race went ahead without Fangio, but even the news that some hotheads had poured oil on the track, causing one car to kill six spectators, didn't take the kidnapping off the front page.

The world's media was focused on this tiny island which had become known, though only dimly in Europe, as a sort of Monaco for Americans.

It was a dream come true for Arnol and his merry gang, but even better news was just around the corner because when Fangio was released, he told waiting newsmen that he had been treated well and that he sympathised with the cause of the rebels.

Amazingly, the great racer stayed in touch with Arnol until the day he died. The kidnapper and the kidnappee became buddies. Weird, hey?

It was certainly very weird to be sitting in the bedroom where Fangio was held, talking to Arnol and knowing that he'd gone on to be Cuba's deputy minister for foreign affairs. I found myself wondering how Terry Waite would feel if one of his abductors were to be seen on TV every night meeting world statesmen like Clinton and Chirac and Gerry Adams.

I didn't exactly worry about it though, because I was beginning to formulate a plan. Whenever I visit a place, I like to bring some permanent reminder home and I was being thwarted at every turn in Havana.

There is almost nothing in the shops, apart from cigars, which I don't like, and shoddy Che Guevara T-shirts. I bought a photocopy of Che's resignation letter to Fidel and even procured a bank note from 1960 signed by beardy himself.

But I wanted something bigger . . . like a car.

The streets really are chock-full of ageing classics which would, with a bit of attention, fetch all sorts of silly prices in the land of MTV.

I'm told that in the current climate, it's hard as hell to get them out but not impossible, and that was good enough. I mean, I'd just seen an Aston Martin DB4 slide by, and I wanted it.

And that Cadillac over there. And the gullwing

Mercedes in that barn. And that Porsche speedster. No kidding, you don't have to hunt for cars like this. They're everywhere.

There was even a Maserati which, said its owner, was one of only two ever made. He didn't know what model it was, and the ravages of time had removed most of the clues, so I wasn't sure whether he was bluffing or not.

This car was a bare shell. It had no engine, no interior trim, no seats, no lights, nothing. But he wanted $50,000 for it, arguing that it had once been used by Mrs Batista, wife of the former president.

This was the third car I'd see that day which had once been used by Mrs Batista, but it was not to be the last. I was shown four Jaguars that had belonged to Frank Sinatra and countless old wrecks which had been vomited in by the old drunk himself, Ernest Hemingway.

Si Señor, I know it is a worthless piece of junk that is not even fit for the scrapyard but Ginger Rogers once owned it so I am asking for $100,000.

And they're not going to give up either, because the haggling has only just begun.

Later, when countless Westerners have told them to get lost, they'll sell for decent money, but not now.

Che Guevara's car was different, though. Here was something that, we know, was used by someone famous. And here it was, after nine days of solid slog, emerging from the old town barn and seeing sunlight for the first time in twenty years.

And there, coming from under the bonnet, were flames. It's strange how one reacts in a situation like this: I did 100 metres in eight seconds as I ran to get the cameraman, so that we could record this momentous event for all time.

Andy, mindful of the budget and how much it would cost us if the damned car burned out completely, behaved rather differently. He dived into a shop, which, miraculously, had some mineral water in the fridge. To the astonishment of the owner, he paid five bucks for one bottle and then poured the contents all over a car which, to the average Cuban, was worth rather less than that.

It worked out quite well in fact. We got some pictures and Andy got the fire out before too much damage was done. The only tragedy was that my drive in this important car was limited to one run down the Malecon seafront.

Communism had wrecked a car. And it has certainly wrecked Cuba, but I guess we were quite lucky really. It never actually got round to wrecking a planet.

Detroit

Way back when, the good people of Detroit decided it would be a good thing to have a railway station. And this was not to be a platform with some geraniums on it either. No siree, you wouldn't be able to find Bernard Cribbins having a chinwag with Jenny Agutter in the steam here. They wanted something big. Really big.

And that's what they got: the biggest, flashiest, tallest railway station the world had ever seen. The huge marble cavern of a concourse sat at the bottom of a twelve-storey skyscraper and backed on to no fewer than sixteen platforms.

Unfortunately, Detroit became the car capital of the world and large, free-flowing urban interstates sprang up like mushrooms after a summer shower. They connected the new suburbs with the downtown auto factories and frankly, no one really needed the station any more.

And so, it closed down.

It's still there, dominating the Detroit skyline, but today it's smashed and broken. Every slab of marble is cracked, the concourse is littered with burned mattresses and the upper floors are said to be in an even worse state of repair.

But no one is absolutely certain because Detroit's railway station is at the end of Michigan Avenue and, as such, is at the epicentre of a gang war that measures 9.4 on the Richter scale.

Rival outfits with silly names like the Ice Warriors fight for control of the high ground. And this is not Reggie and Ronnie Kray either. You can forget all about honour among thieves here. This is vicious like you simply would not believe.

Every year 600 people are shot to death in Detroit and, in that railway station, I very nearly became one of them.

The police had said we were mad to even think about going in there. 'Not even that phoney accent is gonna save your ass. You go in there and you'll come out in a body bag,' said one cheery soul in a hexagonal hat.

But frankly, the British perception of gangland violence is some spotty eleven-year-old with a penknife. We could handle these American pussies, no problem at all.

It took about five minutes to find that we couldn't. We'd just set the camera up when, from the minstrel's gallery, a not-very-minstrel-like voice asked whether we were cops.

We were then ordered to stand still and advised that, if we moved, we would be shot repeatedly. And then killed.

I could have passed muster as a statue until, from behind one of the pillars, came this guy who was about fourteen feet tall and nine feet across. Also, he was brandishing what we later discovered was a 'street sweeper' – a machine gun that fires 12-bore shotgun cartridges.

He frisked us, checked out the camera equipment, listened quite politely while we explained we were from the BBC and then said he was going to check us out.

Now this puzzled me. I was still standing there, wondering if he had a hotline to John Birt, when a girl emerged from the shadows. She last knew what she was doing in 1976. Here was a person whose hair was green, whose nose sported sixteen silver rings and whose eyes had as much life to them as cardboard.

Her first words were odd. 'You're that guy off *Top Gear*, yeah?' 'Um yes,' I replied, wondering where my royalty cheque was if they were showing it in America. Actually, that's a lie. I was really wondering where the lavatory was because I was about four seconds away from shitting myself.

But then her face broke into a broad grin as she explained she'd once worked as a researcher on *Newsnight* and she 'just luurrrved' the BBC.

Within seconds, we were joined by an army of gangland down-and-outs, all clamouring for an interview. Christian, the least stoned and most eloquent, explained that things are pretty bad in downtown Detroit these days.

Had he been shot at? 'What today? Yeah sure. I was down the gas station this morning and these guys came in. It was pretty ugly.'

So we are in danger then? 'You sure are. If they want your trucks, they're going to take 'em. If they want your camera, they're gonna take it. If they want your shoes, you'd better hand 'em over, because if you don't the results could be disappointing. No . . . the results could be catastrophic.'

We had a long chat, turned down several invitations to various parties and left. The police, waiting for us at the end of the drive, were impressed. 'When you went in there we expected you to come out through an eleventh-floor window. How in the hell did you get talking to those guys? You ain't even black,' said one.

Observant bunch, the Detroit cops.

No, they really are. Two days later, we were being driven round an area of the city called Brush which had obviously just been on the receiving end of a B-52 strike. Not a single house was in one piece. Every car in every street was a wreck.

There'd been a drive-by shooting, two people were dead and our chauffeurs were out looking for suspects. It's OK, that's what they were paid to do. They were policemenists.

We were chatting about this and that, about how no one has a job because there are no jobs to be had, when one of them, Hal, suddenly asked if we'd like to see an arrest.

In the blink of an eye, the car had stopped, and two fifteen-year-olds were spread-eagled on the bonnet.

This would have made good footage but sadly, the Chevvy had child locks and we couldn't get out without scrabbling over the front seats and tumbling into the street with my legs tangled up in the umbilical cord that links the camera to the sound equipment.

By the time we were ready to roll, Hal had pulled a small gun and some drugs from the suspects and radioed for back-up . . . which arrived just as the crowd started throwing stones at us.

Another guy was arrested and as he lay on the ground,

his head pinned to the road by Hal's shoe, his friend told cameraman Keith Schofield, 'Get that on your camcorder, Johnnie Fucking Video.'

This was getting ugly and we already knew that everyone was packing heat. You can buy a gun in Detroit for less than half a dozen tomatoes and the statistics show that a gun is a lot more useful.

I must confess that I kept staring at the tiny pistol that had been confiscated earlier and was now lying on the passenger seat of the police car. Was it loaded? Where was the safety catch? Had anyone in the crowd started firing, you should be in no doubt that I'd have fired back.

And I'm the guy who had to lie in a cold room for three days after I once shot a sparrow with an air rifle.

Happily, we emerged from the confrontation in one piece, even though our Chrysler Town and Country people carrier had taken a direct hit.

Compared to Detroit, the rest of America is Trumpton. You ask an American if he's ever been there and he'll be too flabbergasted to answer. You can buy T-shirts elsewhere in the States which say things like 'Don't Mess With Me. I Have Friends In Detroit' or 'DETROIT – Where The Weak Are Killed And Eaten'.

That's strange because, just 30 years ago, Detroit was the most vibrant city America had ever seen. The people were rich. The factories were humming. You could hear the buzz all round the world. So what turned the motor capital of the world into the murder capital of the world?

Well, way back at the dawn of automotive time, and seemingly quite by chance, a number of individuals set up shop in and around De Troit (it used to be French) making cars. A great many covered wagons had been built there and the city simply added the newfangled internal combustion engine.

This city was home base to Lincoln, Cadillac, Pontiac, Chevrolet, Ford, Mercury, Chrysler, Hudson, Plymouth, Buick, Dodge, Packard and Oldsmobile. It was The Motor City.

There were more car-makers than people and, to attract workers from elsewhere in the States, the pay was high. By the late fifties, the average industrial wage rate in America was $1.50 an hour but in Detroit they were getting $3.

You could start work in one factory on a Monday morning and, if you didn't like it, catch the afternoon shift in another later that day.

Demand was phenomenal, too. These were the US boom years, before the oil crisis, Vietnam and Watergate, and everyone wanted a car: a big one with a V8 engine from Detroit. In the fifties and sixties, 97 per cent of all cars sold in America were made in America.

No car sums up the times better than the original 1964 Mustang. This two-door saloon was an adventurous departure, not only for Ford but for the whole car industry.

Until the Mustang came along, every car had a specific engine and a specific level of luxury. There was no choice. But with the 'pony car', as it became known, customers could choose what motor they wanted and even what body style – two-door saloon or convertible.

And there was an options list. You could go for bucket

seats, for instance, or a limited slip differential or a rev counter. It could be a 6-cylinder shopping car or a V8 wind-in-the-hair tyre-shredder.

Ford guessed they were on to something with this new idea and reckoned they'd sell 100,000 Mustangs in the first twelve months. In fact, they sold 680,000 making it the fastest-selling car of all time – a record that's never been beaten.

But today, the only records being made are crime statistics.

So what went wrong? Well, most importantly, there was the oil crisis which made people slightly less willing to run a V8 with its Oliver-Reedesque thirst. They wanted smaller engines and turned their attention to the new-fangled Japanese offerings.

And hey, these cars never broke down, so even when the oil problem went away many stuck with Honda and Datsun and Toyota.

Then there was assembly-line automation, which was bad enough, but cheap land prices didn't help either.

When the car company wanted to update a factory, it didn't simply put in a robot here and a conveyor belt there. No, it shut up shop completely and built a new plant, usually out of town where land was cheaper.

Detroit might have been able to cope with all these things but unfortunately there was economic trouble in the South and thousands of black workers were heading to Detroit in a fruitless search for work. They'd heard about the promise of three bucks an hour but when they got there, the cupboard was bare.

Social unrest was inevitable. In 1967, the African-Americans took to the streets and had themselves the riot to end all riots.

Bob Seger, who at the time was an up-and-coming rock and roller from Detroit, remembers coming home from a gig one night to find tanks on the streets. 'I just couldn't believe it. This was Detroit and the whole place was on fire. There were police everywhere. They'd got the national guard out. It was like a war zone. It was worse than a war zone. It was hell.'

Shortly after, the White Flight began, as respectable middle-class white families packed up and moved to the suburbs, where half the factories had gone anyway.

In ten years, the population of Detroit halved from two million to one million. Even the Motown record label, which had made Detroit a world capital of music too with its wealth of black artists like Stevie Wonder, Martha Reeves, Diana Ross and the Temptations, moved to Los Angeles.

They weren't 'Dancing in the Streets' any more. Madonna may have been born there but she left, too.

And that was it. Detroit became a wrecked shell whose population is still falling. There are no jobs downtown today and when Hudson's, the big department store, closed down, most of the city-centre retailers followed suit and went under too.

It's hard for a European to understand this because we have no equivalent, but there is a very real possibility that one day, Detroit will implode: that it will simply cease to exist.

Already, there are people in the suburbs who are proud to say they haven't been downtown in twenty years. The nineteen-year-old doorman at our hotel in Dearborn admitted one night he'd *never* been there.

He simply couldn't believe it when, every morning, we bundled our kit into the trucks and went off to the centre, even though it was only twelve miles away. He was even more amazed, though, when we actually came back each night.

He obviously had a word with the manager who, one day, advised us not to go down there any more. When he found that we had to and that we preferred to drive in on Michigan Avenue, rather than down the safer expressway, he rushed off to explain to the girls on the reception desk that our rooms might become available sooner than he'd thought.

Despite this attitude, the mayor, Dennis Archer, is ebullient, saying that Detroit was only murder capital of the world once and that no one will beat the city in making quality cars. 'We'll take on anyone, any time,' he crows.

But he's missing the point because none of the car firms is dependent on Detroit any more. GM has a factory in Mexico for chrissakes. Honda is in Marysville, Ohio. Toyota and BMW have factories in the USA too, but they're not even in Michigan.

Sure, Ford, GM and Chrysler – the only remaining US car firms – still build cars on their home turf, but they're in the leafy suburbs. And when I say leafy, I'm talking equatorial rainforest.

Should you ever need to go to Detroit, drive west from

the city centre on Jefferson, past Belle Isle and make sure your windows are up. Crash the red lights too, because to stop here is to invite the unwelcome intrusion of a 9-mm slug.

And then, at one set of lights, you'll notice that everything changes. On the east side, the shops are burned out and shabby. Black men shuffle around in the wreckage looking for anything that could be lunch – a bedspring or a butt end, perhaps.

On the other side of the lights, the fire hydrants are painted Dulux commercial white, the street lamps are mock Tudor and the houses are immaculate and huge. Every fourth car is a police cruiser and every third person is out jogging. Welcome to Grosse Point, a lakeside suburb where the big car-firm bosses live.

I hated it. This was like something out of *The Stepford Wives* and we'd only been there for five minutes when the cops arrived. They'd had a flood of calls about a group of guys in jeans. Jeans in Grosse Point. You'd get further in a G-string at Henley.

I swear that before we left we even saw someone cutting his lawn with a pair of nail scissors.

It's not quite so bad on the other side of the city, north of Eight Mile Road which is the accepted barrier between rich and poor, black and white, civilisation and a Bronze Age war zone.

These are just like any American suburbs – until the Friday-night reminder that you're in The Motor City. Or near it anyway.

There's a pretty vibrant classic-car scene out there as car

workers past and present feel the need to restore and pamper great cars from the days when their city was great too. They meet up at weekends with their customised, power-packed Chevvies and Fords and discuss each other's sometimes spectacular beards over a Bud or two.

They even have their own radio station called Honey which is run from the back of a four-wheel-drive truck. It simply turns up at the meeting and plays a selection of good old rock and roll.

I'll tell you this. Wandering around a car park full of hot Mustangs and lowered Vettes on a hot summer's night with Bob Seger belting out of a couple of hundred car radios takes some beating.

What beat it was what happened when AJ's Lounge and Eaterie closed. These guys didn't simply get into their cars and go home. No, they got in, eased out onto the road alongside each other, waiting for the lights to go green and had a race.

All over suburban Detroit every summer weekend every straight bit of road echoes to the sound of supercharged V8s doing full-bore standing quarters.

Big money changes hands. Bets of up to a thousand dollars are not unknown as the cars line up . . . on the public roads.

You can barely see through the haze of tyre smoke as El Camino pickups roar off the line at full revs. Wilbur and Myrtle can only stare in open-mouthed wonderment as their puny little Honda finds itself sandwiched between a lime-green Dodge Charger and an egg-yellow Plymouth Super Bird.

This is as subtle as a Big Mac, as restrained as a can of Coke and as American as both. Big cars, big engines, big people and big beards, racing each other over a quarter of a mile straightaway.

These guys spit at Ferraris and laugh at Lotus Elans. They are not interested in a car's ability to handle the bends on a switchback mountain pass. They don't care about pinball-sharp steering or five-valve technology.

They'd drink a pint of warm beer before they'd own up to a fondness for European and Japanese engines that rev to 8000 rpm.

They like their V8s big and lazy and their rear tyres massive. American street racing is straight down the line and simple. It's a national characteristic. The only thing in the world less complex than a blue-collar American is wood.

One guy watched a bright-blue Camaro launch itself off the line with its front tyres a foot in the air, then turned to me grinning and said, 'Chevrolets and apple pie, baby, Chevrolets and apple pie.'

It didn't make sense but I knew exactly what he meant. This was heartland America.

And the cops were not about to make waves, partly because they need the support of the white middle classes. A patrol car sat for an hour in a side street watching the action before moving in.

Over the car's public address system he announced that the show was over and that 'anyone on the street in ten minutes is going to jail'. It would have been terribly authoritarian and effective except for one thing. I could see through the tyre smoke and the flashing lights that the guy was grinning.

He knew that he was witnessing what the people of Detroit have been doing for 50 years.

In the sixties, manufacturers used to bring secret new cars down to these meets and race them against the home-tuned opposition. Many remember Ford rolling up one night in the early seventies with some kind of Mustang which blew everyone into the weeds. It became the Mach 1.

It's stories like this which set Detroit apart. It doesn't matter where you turn, there is always a reminder that you are in The Motor City.

There's a comic book sold locally where all the heroes are cars. Take a stroll round the Detroit Institute of Arts which, amazingly, still exists downtown, and you'll note that every single exhibit was paid for and is funded by the car industry.

The poets in Detroit write about cars and within a twenty-mile radius of the city-centre grand prix track there are five drag strips. Ben Hamper, a local boy and the funniest author I've ever read, is a former GM worker.

And downtown, there are the buildings, huge and solid monoliths whose foundations are set in V8 brawn. Pick any one of them and you'll find it was built with car-industry money. They're the American equivalent of Britain's country houses, a solid and lingering reminder of a once-great past.

And an inspiration to strive for a better future. The American car industry has owned up to the fact that the

Japanese were an invented enemy dreamed up to disguise its own shortcomings and has now stopped making awful cars.

Sure, there's still the Buick Skylark and the Chevrolet Caprice, brontosaurial machines which handle like lawn-mowers and have all the visual appeal of dog dirt. But at least they're well made these days.

American cars, from the seventies especially, were not only hideous to behold but they were also prone to cata-strophic bouts of unhelpfulness. It was not uncommon to find Coke cans rattling in the doors and a line worker's tuna sandwiches under the seat.

And GM's answer to poor morale was to introduce the Quality Cat, a man in a moggy outfit who bounded up and down the lines, inspiring a cynical workforce to greater things. Trouble is, most of them were asleep in boxes at the time, or down at the shop-rat's bar.

Ben Hamper tells the story of new electronic boards which were erected throughout the factory. One day, the message read 'Riveting is fun', which made him ask the question, 'Well hey, if it's so good, how come all the management aren't coming down here in their lunch breaks to have a go?'

Those days though are long gone and even the designers are back on form with cars like the Dodge Viper, the Lincoln Mark VIII and the Saturn range. They're good-looking, inexpensive, reliable and advanced. The Cadillac STS only needs servicing every 100,000 miles and, thanks to sophisticated electronics, can cross a desert with no water in the radiator.

But if you want to spotlight one car which demonstrates Detroit's new spirit, you should take a look at the Chrysler LHS.

It's made by a company which, in the early eighties, was teetering on the verge of bankruptcy but which is now posting profits which some say are obscene.

Most American cars are too large, too thirsty and too ugly to have any appeal outside the States but the LHS is different. It looks wonderful, thanks to its cab-forward design whereby the engine is shoved right up to the front of the engine bay.

That lets you have a short bonnet which means more space for passengers and luggage. It's also quiet, well-equipped and fast, despite the absence of a V8 motor. I'm almost embarrassed to say it but here we have a car which, by global standards, is right up there with the best.

It, along with the new Fords and GM cars, means that in the short term, at least, the big three American car manufacturers are safe. But what about their birth town? What about Detroit?

Well there are some chinks of light. Today, right in the city centre, there is one 300-yard stretch called Greektown where trendy restaurants abound and where you can walk on the pavement at night in relative safety. There are lots of beggars but they only let murderers in in packs of ten.

There is also the appropriately named Renaissance Center, which houses office blocks, a shopping mall and the world's tallest hotel. You're fairly safe in there too because armed guards outnumber visitors by 200 to 1.

And there's the people mover – a monorail which tours

the city. Now sure, it's pretty pointless offering a public transport alternative in a city where the public don't go and where, even if they did, they'd take a car, but never mind; someone had the confidence to build such a thing.

The trouble is, these are details. Building a shiny new monorail in Detroit is like cutting someone's toenails when they have lung cancer. And Detroit, to pinch a line from *Robocop*, does have cancer.

It's called crime.

The Mayor says Detroit will be the next great international city, and a great place to do business. Yes, and I'm a little teapot.

I'm so mad, in fact, that I always list Detroit as one of my five favourite cities in the world. It is as soulful as the music it once made and, as Gertrude Stein once said, 'There is a *there* there'.

Iceland

Iceland is not of this earth. It is a little piece of Mars stuck away on a barren rock in the middle of the North Atlantic. There are no reference points for the visitor, no little reminders of the civilisation that you've left behind, no clues that you're in a fully paid-up NATO member state. Small wonder they sent Neil Armstrong here to train for his lunar walk.

The countryside is weird. The people are mad. The weather defies belief and the laws and customs leave you gasping. But all of this is overshadowed by one important feature that, quite literally, turns your world upside down. In the summer, it doesn't go dark.

They can take you for a ride in a nitro-powered Jeep up a sheer cliff face. You can drive a snowmobile across the sea. You can pay £80 for a bottle of house white and you can have dinner with a girl who has completely see-through skin, but you won't be paying attention because here, night does not necessarily follow day.

Life for the rest of Planet Earth is a mishmash of unpredictability but there's always one inescapable fact – every single night, without fail, the sun *will* set.

But up there, from the end of April to the middle of September, night is like easing the dimmer switch down a couple of notches. And in the middle of June, it doesn't happen at all.

At three or four o'clock in the morning, it's as light as it was at three or four o'clock in the afternoon, and that is spooky. You can go up to Sneffels Yokul, where Arne Saknussem set off in *Journey to the Center of the Earth*, to watch the sun kiss the horizon, and then start rising again.

Not surprisingly, this peculiar aspect of life in the far north has had an effect on the people who live there. They don't behave like human beings. If Darwin had come here instead of the Galápagos Islands, he'd have deduced that, on the evolutionary scale, man followed on from the hedgehog.

In the summer months, the Icelander doesn't really do much sleeping. And at weekends, he doesn't do any at all.

When they finish work in Reykjavik on a Friday night, they go home, have some drinks, get changed, have some more drinks and then at 11.00 p.m. they go out: all 125,000 of them.

This can be a bit of a shock if you've arrived from Earth. The first time I went there, ten years ago, I wandered around at eightish looking for a restaurant, not really surprised that the streets were deserted. This, after all, was the northernmost capital city in the world and it was a bit chilly.

But as I sat with a plate of fish and coleslaw, I couldn't help noticing that as the night wore on, the tables were filling up, and then some. By midnight, there were queues of expectant diners going right out of the door.

So I took out a mortgage, paid up and left, whereupon I was thrust into the world's biggest party. If you could combine Live Aid with a papal visit to Rio, you'd get something that, compared to this, was a village fête.

Everyone was hog-whimperingly drunk. As Björk put it recently, 'What's the point of having a glass of wine every day? It's a waste of money, a waste of time and waste of wine. Why not wait till the weekend and drink a litre of vodka all in one go?'

So they do. The teenagers, those too young to get into the endless array of nightclubs, fill massive Coke bottles with nine parts vodka and one part Coke and get so pissed most of them walk round backwards.

And then, if they're girls, they get pregnant. Iceland has the highest rate of illegitimacy in the world because most teenage girls have a child at sixteen which is then brought up by their parents. They are then free to have a life without worrying about the biological clock. They say Bangkok is the sex capital of the world: it isn't – not by a long way.

And nor is Monaco the epicentre of partydom. Reykjavik has that one all sewn up, too.

The gathering, which starts on a Friday at midnight, goes on until Monday morning when people go directly from their disco to work. It's bizarre but they really do seem to have developed sleep patterns based on the tortoise. You're awake for six months, and then you're not.

Anyone planning to invade Iceland would be advised to hit the beaches some time between November and

February because no one's awake. Mind you, you could go in June too because everyone is rat-faced.

Everyone, that is, except the huge gangs of bikers that roam the streets at night with massive Mad Maxian hogs and biblical hairdos. 'What,' I asked nervously, 'do you do?'

I expected them to say they barbecued virgins and danced naked in front of ceremonial fires but this was not quite the case. 'Oh,' said one. 'We campaign for safer roads and lower insurance rates. That sort of thing.'

How come you're all sober? 'Let me make one thing absolutely plain here,' said another, who was wearing a US tank-driver's helmet. 'No one in Iceland drinks and drives. You see, this is a small community and if you get pissed and knock someone down, there's a strong chance you will know them. And if you don't know them, it is absolutely certain that you will know someone who does.'

And feeling duty-bound to go to the funeral of someone who you killed is, well, a little embarrassing.

For the same reason, you can leave your car and your house unlocked. When I asked a policeman how much car crime there is in Iceland, he genuinely didn't know what I was on about.

So you have more time to worry about murder then? And that got him too. In Iceland, in the last ten years, there have only been a dozen cases of homicide and most of those were crimes of passion – the type where Plod arrives to find the wife dead and the husband sobbing away in a corner, smoking gun in hand and explaining to anyone who will listen that he didn't mean to kill her.

It's not all sweetness and light, though. For the most

part, people are pleased to welcome foreigners who've come to do something other than fish, but there's a significant number who reckon you're gate-crashing their party.

They're living up there, on their funny rock, having a ball in a crime-free, stable and fantastically rich country and they don't want yobbos from the real world sticking their noses in. More than once I was told to 'fuck off back to America'.

I stayed though, because Iceland is my kinda town.

It is four-fifths the size of England but they have the biggest glacier in the northern hemisphere, 100 active volcanoes and rivers that change course every day. There are no trees and it's not unknown for new islands to spring up off the coast from time to time.

Iceland is located right where the American and European continental shelves meet and that makes it the world's biggest geothermal playground too.

A lot of the rock in Iceland is warm to the touch because, just a few hundred feet below the surface, it's still molten. Steam pours out of the ground and huge chunks of the place smell worse than the Japanese underground on a bad day.

Then there's the blue lagoon. Not far from the main airport at Keflavik, where the American air force is based, you'll find a hot lake of the most improbable turquoise. Below the surface, things go even more bonkers. Here the water is so hot that the whole country gets free baths, central heating and power without having to burn a single hydrocarbon.

One man told me that Iceland has enough free and eco-friendly power under its surface to keep Western Europe going for a thousand years. Then he fell off his bar stool.

And then there's the town of Geyser which has given its name, the world over, to a huge water spout. The great geyser hasn't strutted its stuff for years but there is a selection of smaller ones that gurgle and slurp away most of the time and, every seven minutes, shoot a plume of boiling water 70 feet into the air. It would be quite a sight in, say, Barnsley, but in Iceland you might even call it dull.

This is because to get there, you'll have driven past Gull Foss, a waterfall of such drama and power that your ears start to bleed. My eyebrows went green too.

Then there's the spongy moss which has turned a monster lava field into the world's biggest mattress, the black desert and the complete absence of agriculture. Eighty per cent of Iceland's mad interior is common land, given to the people by the world's oldest parliament.

And remember, I'm talking here about a people who sleep all winter and party all summer, a people who, by any sense of the word, are crazy.

They just don't play by the same rules as the rest of the world. There is no Icelandic word for 'please'. Until very recently, beer was banned, even though spirits were not. There was no television on Thursdays. They don't even have proper surnames.

When you're born, you are given a name by your parents, which is normal enough except it must come from a government-approved list.

Your surname is your father's Christian name with 'son' or 'dottir' tacked on the end. So, I would be called Jeremy Edwardson and my daughter, Emily Jeremydottir.

Weird stuff, but not as weird as the prices. In 1994, when we were there, petrol was nearly £5 a gallon. A bottle of wine in a pizza joint was £65 and dinner for two in one of the endless fish restaurants cost the same as four television licence fees. I've framed my hotel bill and it now hangs in the hall to amuse visitors.

The national pastime up there, apart from going to the bank twice a day, is statistics. Chat to an Icelander for more than a minute and you'll learn that they've produced more chess grand masters and Miss Worlds than any other nation on earth. But this is not surprising because all the men have beards and look like Nordic facsimiles of Greek philosophers, and the women look like angels. Björk is the only one who's odd, and they've exported her.

But you need to delve into their motoring culture to get the real picture – to see just how mad this place is. Take a look in the history books to see what I mean.

The first car arrived on Icelandic soil in 1904 but with no infrastructure and no spare parts it soon died. However, rather than simply throw it away, its owner would push it up a hill and charge inquisitive visitors a small fee for the privilege of rolling down to the bottom in it.

There was even a car factory once. Back in 1941, a ship carrying 104 kits was on its way from America to Sweden, where they would be made into Dodge saloons, when it became stranded in Iceland because of the war.

An Icelandic mechanic was dispatched to the States to get a job in the Dodge factory while a small factory was built in Reykjavik. By the time it was ready, he knew how the cars were made and he did just that in less than a year. Sadly, in rather less time than that, most had been eaten by the winter weather so that today only one remains in active service . . . as a chicken run.

Then there's motorsport which, until recently, was impossible because road-traffic laws applied everywhere. You could have built a racetrack but it would have been subjected to the blanket 70kph speed limit.

However, in 1981, they changed the law and Iceland went motorsport barmy, to the point that today, every weekend, central Iceland echoes to the sound of what are by far the most powerful race cars in the known world.

To the casual observer, they're Jeeps, but this is like calling a Michelin three-star lunch a snack.

They have Detroit V8 engines and four-wheel drive, but that's about all they have in common with what you see cruising up and down the King's Road on a Saturday. The tyres, for a kickoff, are two feet wide and equipped with scoop-like flaps to give extra grip. The chassis are massively altered too, elongated and beefed up so that they stay in one piece after a 100-foot drop.

Then there are the engines, which must be capable of getting the car up the 100-foot climb in the first place. They are, basically, tuned V8s of 5- or 7-litre capacity but, for that little extra something, when you hit the gas hard, ultra-cold nitrous oxide is brought into play, giving a total of 900 horsepower.

To put that in perspective, Michael Shoemaker's Benetton develops somewhere in the region of 600 bhp. These Icelandic Jeeps are absolutely terrifying, a point that was hammered home when Gisli Jonsson, the current champion, took me out for a spin.

The course is laid out over what, in Britain, we'd call a quarry. And what you do is drive up the walls, the idea being that the first part of the climb is nearly vertical and the last ten to twelve feet, completely sheer. And you get no run-up.

Once at the top, you turn round, come halfway down again and then, turn round on a slope that looks virtually vertical, crab along it and then go straight up again. To describe it as impossible is to underestimate the seriousness of the task.

Gisli agreed that some of the slopes were, indeed, out of the question, but added, 'We'll give them a try anyway.' Then he hit three-quarter power and with the wheels spinning like a washing machine on its final spin cycle we rocketed skywards. And, as the front wheels hit the vertical part of the wall, his right foot welded the pedal to the metal, the nitro kicked in, my kidneys exploded and whoosh, we were at the top.

Except 'whoosh' is the wrong word. I have stood underneath a hovering Harrier. I have heard a brace of Tornadoes do a combat-power military take off. I've seen Judas Priest live and I've been in a Formula One pit when they've taken a V10 to 17,000 rpm, but these sounds are whisper-quiet compared to Gisli's Jeep. We're talking bird song at the World Pile-Driver Competition.

With such a massive assault being mounted on one sense, the others go into shutdown, which is a good thing because my eyes simply refused to believe what was happening.

I'd been told that the nitro needs to come in at the exact moment the rear wheels hit the vertical part of the slope, causing them to bounce away from the rock face and thus, hopefully, causing the car to rock over the lip. It didn't make much sense at the time and having done it, it makes even less now.

But there was worse to come. On the way down, Gisli swung the wheel over to the left so that we drove across this sheer rock face.

He had no gear-changing to worry about – it's auto-matic – but even so, things often go wrong. Cars roll down the banks all the time but that said, in ffiteen years, no competitor has ever been injured. This, frankly, was cold comfort, because I was scared out of my mind – and I'm talking about scared in the bowel-loosening sense. The last time that someone was this scared, he was about eight and he was having a nightmare about some headless monsters eating his mum and dad.

Three things stopped me from asking Gisli to stop. First, I'm British. Second, I couldn't make myself heard. And third, I was sitting on my arms to stop them flailing about if we rolled. So I simply sat there, wishing to God that I was an accountant.

And then it was over and I went for a ride on a Yamaha Wave Runner.

Nothing odd in that. You did it a hundred times when

you were on holiday. Aha. But have you done it in an Icelandic lake, while wearing jeans? No? I thought not.

There was a bit of a wind and, therefore, because it was a big lake, a bit of a chop, but there was nothing to warn me about what was to come. What came the first time I hit a wave hard was a series of large icicles which ploughed into my face, at exactly the same time that a sub-zero fist took hold of my genitals and squeezed. This was cold like you simply would not believe.

'Yes,' said my Icelandic guide later. 'Ten people died of hypothermia last year after they fell in there.'

Worse was to come when he introduced me to the fantastically named Sudberdur Gudbergson who, two years ago, rode his snowmobile to an island 1.2 km off the coast. Now, it should be explained at this juncture that a snowmobile is designed for use on water in a rather more solid state. A snowmobile has all the buoyancy of a cathedral. If you put a snowmobile on water, you will need a new snowmobile, and in Iceland, that would cost about the same as Blenheim Palace.

Sudberdur Gudbergson's would cost even more because it is tuned to develop 180 bhp, which makes it more powerful than your Golf GTi. In terms of power to weight, it is more powerful than a Lamborghini Diablo.

To make it suitable for use on water, Sud, as I shall call him, had simply taped over the radiator grilles – overheating is rarely a problem in Iceland – and that was it. 'Have a go,' he said, 'only remember that, no matter what, keep it on full power. If you lift off for a second, she will go down.'

Now, I rode it up and down the beach a couple of times and discovered that flat out equated to about 120 mph, which was awesome enough on dry land. Could there be something more terrifying than Gisli's Jeep?

Yes.

To begin with I kept to the shallows, which enabled me to learn that the two skis up front are no substitute for a rudder and the tank track at the back is not really a very good propeller.

But what the hell. I swung it round, hit a max and plunged onto the water on a course that would take me right across to the other side of the lake, half a mile away. The speed started to bleed off immediately and the skidoo began to rock from side to side but I knew that to lift my thumb from the throttle would mean a loss in momentum and frozen knackers all over again.

I guess I was down to about 50 mph halfway across when the strangest thing happened. Gisli came past in his Jeep. I'm not kidding. I felt pretty manly and hirsute on my lightweight skidoo but here was a man driving his 900-bhp Jeep on water.

They tried to explain the physics of it later but frankly, I kept trying to match the man's face with the boat race on the Turin shroud. I guess if Jesus wanted to come to earth again for a bit of a poke around, Iceland makes sense – lots of fishing, no one bats an eyelid when you walk on water, bikers who look like disciples anyway. It's the perfect cover.

And should Pilot Pontiusson come round with some centurions, lots of places to hide.

Iceland's interior is deserted, by which I mean no crofter's huts, no pylons, no people. Think about that. Imagine being able to go from Newcastle upon Tyne to Oxford without seeing any evidence at all of man's existence. This is one big chunk of nature.

And the biggest chunk of the lot is the glacier. Vatna-jokull is bigger than Yorkshire.

I guess it's time to get all *Blue Peter*-ish now and explain that you can't simply drive onto this kilometre-thick chunk of ice all on your own. You need guides, satellite navigation equipment and some very, very special vehicles.

They're basically big four-wheel-drive vans which have been described by one American magazine as the best snow vehicles in the world, and you can't argue with that, as they cruise over crevices so deep that mammoths still live at the bottom. You also can't argue when you see how much they cost – £60,000 is by no means uncommon.

I should explain that every square metre of Iceland has been plotted and, with the right satnav equipment, you can drive across the middle in a car with blacked-out windows.

But a glacier moves. Your pet satellite can tell you which way you're going but not what's between you and your destination. It's no good thinking, as you plummet down a kilometre-deep crack, 'That's odd. This wasn't here yesterday.'

Plus, you need to be mindful of the weather. Not even in the uppermost reaches of Scotland's taller bits will you find changeable conditions like this. You can be sunbathing one minute and dead the next. We're a few miles from the Arctic Circle here and they have blizzards which would give Michael Fish a heart attack. Sometimes, they're even more powerful than his jackets.

So why, then, do Icelanders bother to go up there? Well, first of all, they're mad, and second, they go because there's no reason not to.

Why, for instance, go into the African bush when there's a better-than-evens chance of not getting out with all your legs on? Why climb Everest and why, in British terms, have a barbecue when you have an oven?

The first thing you do before hitting the ice is drop the tyre pressure down to just two pounds per square inch, so that the rubber makes a bigger footprint on the snow. And don't worry about it coming off the wheel because you only need a Zippo and some lighter fluid to put it back on again. What you do is spray the butane into the tyre and light it. The resultant explosion pops the tyre back on the rim and gives just enough pressure to carry on. And carry on you must because journey's end is a huge slash in the ice.

And to give you an idea about how huge, you could play hide-and-seek in there with Canary Wharf and not find it.

I don't want to get all religious here but when you stand on the edge of this absurd crater you do start to wonder a little bit about the puniness of man. I mean, not even the most powerful nuclear bomb could do this. The power that created it is beyond the ken of even our most sophisticated computer. We really are pretty pathetic and I suppose that if I lived near it, and all Iceland's other wonders, I might have a slightly lower opinion of myself.

Perhaps this is why Icelanders, more than anyone else I've ever met, live so close to the edge.

Either that or they have the fishing industry to thank. I mean, if a country relies for its huge wealth on fish, which can only be caught by ploughing the North Atlantic in small boats, playtime is going to be pretty special.

I also think, though, that quite by chance we'd stumbled on a nation that simply likes cars. Certainly, it's hard to see the internal combustion engine as a threat to mankind up there.

When you stand in a normal city street, and the whole thing is clogged up with tail pipes, smoky buses and the interminable din from a million diesels, it's easy to see why the environmental argument can get a toehold.

But in Iceland, one exhaust pipe on a glacier the size of Yorkshire doesn't seem so bad.

Then we have the queues. It's easy to see the appeal of public transport in Britain where every motorway is clogged, and every B-road alternative a washboard route directly to the osteopath.

They have queues in Iceland too, but never so severely that you'd think about taking the bus instead. And anyway, you can always call the transport minister whose number – and that of the President herself – appears in the phonebook.

'Oh people call me up all the time,' he says. 'If there's the slightest problem, they're straight on the phone to me. This is a small place and everyone knows everyone else.

Just because you work in the transport ministry doesn't mean you stop knowing people.'

The transport ministry needs to be defined though. Put it like this. When he goes out for lunch, it's closed.

Sure, he has the planes, the buses and the cars to worry about but, thankfully, no trains. There are none.

However, outside California, Iceland does have the highest car-ownership levels in the world and the roads have to keep pace with a demand that just won't slow down.

To cope, they have Road One, which circumnavigates Iceland and is paved for very nearly its entire length. The best stretch is in the south where you'll find the Big Bridge which was paid for by Iceland's lottery and is fashioned from wood – odd in a country without any trees. Well there used to be some, but the original Irish settlers – Reg and Vic – chopped them all down.

There is no Road Two but there is a myriad of unnumbered and unpaved tracks which litter the coastal plains. On these you should be very, very careful indeed because Iceland's growing band of rally drivers use them for practice in their homemade cars.

In Britain they'd call it joy-riding and the transport minister would appear on television with a stern face. But hey, this is Iceland and the transport minister thinks it's OK so long as they're careful.

He's also not that bothered by the microlighting fraternity, who simply land on what, in Britain, would be the M1, and pull into a service station for petrol. 'Well where else would I get gas?' said one.

You sometimes get the impression that the Icelandic parliament is rather like a parish council presiding over a piece of geological lunacy, but it's not. Iceland is in NATO and is a European state, even if they've had the good sense to keep the EC at bay.

They really have worked out a different way of life up there and it works a damn sight better than every other country I've ever been to. Iceland, as far as I'm concerned, is simply the best.

I wasn't even slightly surprised to find that Reykjavik is chock-full of ex-pat Britishers who went there for a holiday once and decided not to come home. Ask them why and you always get the same answer. 'What? Are you kidding!'

They may moan about the agonising price of everything and the desperation of living through an Icelandic winter, but they know they're at the best party in town, and they're not coming home.

Indeed, when you're in Iceland, you tend to look out on the rest of the world through shit-coloured spectacles.

Iceland is God's finest hour.

Japan

When you wake up in a Japanese hotel bedroom after a fourteen-hour flight across the international date line, you get an idea of how Dave Bowman felt at the end of *2001: A Space Odyssey*.

Yes, it is a hotel room with a bed, a dressing table, a television and a wardrobe. The bathroom looks normal too, right down to the fan that will not shut down unless you hit it with a hammer.

But there are little clues which suggest that this is a facsimile of a real hotel room. The carpet, for instance, is the same shade of purple as a pair of loons I had back in 1971. The easy chair is button-back and finished in ice-white plastic. None of the food listed in the room service menu is recognisable as such. I wanted bacon and eggs. I got a Thai green curry.

Then there's the telephone. Not once during my two-week stay did I ever work it out. I think I once managed to get through to someone in England, but it sure as hell wasn't my wife. Mostly, I ended up talking to hotel laundry boys, who'd scuttle into my room moments later, sweeping up all the clothes I'd planned to wear that day.

And I'd run after them, saying 'no' a lot and looking ridiculous because the hotel-issue dressing gown did about as much to protect my modesty as one of Colin Moynahan's cardigans.

Generally speaking, international hotels have a re-markable knack of erasing any clues about what country you're in. They've tried in Japan too, but they've failed. Miserably.

In one hotel there, in Kyoto, there was a different pair of slippers laid out in each of the suite's many rooms. However, as they were of a size that would have given a baby blisters, I just clomped around in my cowboy boots. It's also worth mentioning that in this hotel bedroom, there was one huge ingredient missing – a bed. Also, none of the tables or chairs had legs, and the bath was made of wood.

Even the television wasn't normal. It doesn't matter where you go on the planet, you always get CNN which rattles through world events in eight seconds and then does a two-hour, in-depth report on the plight of potato farmers in Idaho. The presenters look like they're from outer space too, with their wild, staring eyes and their hurricane-proof hairdos.

But in Japan, I couldn't get CNN, or BBC World or MTV or anything in English, which may sound arrogant but is, in fact, unusual. So I had to resort to local breakfast TV which is like nothing on earth. Men in suits lean forwards when reading the news and shout.

And if it isn't the news, it's a kung-fu movie where people hit each other a lot. I speak no foreign languages but can usually work out what's going on when watching alien TV. But the programme I found that morning seemed to be a cross between *Crimewatch* and *Dangermouse*.

It was hopeless and anyway, it was time to go to work, which, that day, involved going to Mazda's research and development centre fifteen miles away in Yokohama.

The lobby was huge, really gigantic and there was more purple carpeting. But stranger still, all the white plastic button-backed chairs were arranged in rows, like in an airport departure lounge. It felt about as welcoming as the cold storage room at an abattoir, so I met up with the equally bewildered crew and left.

Or tried to. The doors slid back electrically but were flanked by two porters who, as they opened, bowed. It was very charming, flattering even, but their heads were touching and there was no way past.

So I said 'excuse me' and they bowed a bit lower. Another 'excuse me' and they began to look like pre-pubescent Russian gymnasts, only smaller. One more 'excuse me' did it. The bows became so pronounced that their heads touched their knees and we were able to slip through.

And into real trouble. There are 121 million people in Japan and nearly all of them were porters at our hotel. As a guest, you aren't allowed to do anything, even tip, which is embarrassing as these guys, some of whom were only three inches tall, struggled to manhandle 200 kg of camera and lighting equipment into our Mitsubishi Super Exceed people carrier. Crazy name. Crazy car.

This was to be the crew's transport while the production team was to be chauffeur-driven by our man on the ground in a Mitsubishi Debonair, a car that was anything but.

It was very large when you looked at it from the outside but absolutely microscopic when you climbed on to one of its button-backed plastic chairs. This is because of all the equipment they'd shovelled inside. Who needs leg room when you can have a dash-mounted television screen that doubles up as a map of Tokyo?

It's clever, this. The on-board satellite navigation processor works out exactly where you are and a small arrow points to a particular point on the map. You can then tell it where you want to go, and it works out a route – vital in a city like Tokyo which is 50 miles across.

And unlike any other large conurbation, there are no architectural changes as you move from area to area. In London, there's no way you could confuse Cricklewood with Soho or Kensington with Docklands, but in Tokyo it all looks exactly the same – grey, cramped and, usually, wet. It's a symphony of concrete and neon, *Bladerunner* meets Bedlam. It is hell on earth. To say that I hate Tokyo more than anywhere else in the world is to understate the point badly.

Still, today I was going to look upon it from the air-conditioned splendour of my Mitsubishi Debonair which, at eight o'clock in the morning, was trying to get out of the hotel car park.

At nine o'clock, it was still trying to get out of the hotel car park and there was no blood in my legs.

At ten past ten, the traffic jam moved a bit and we were off . . . by which I mean we were off hotel property and onto the road network. Four hours later, the fifteen-mile journey was over and we found ourselves on an industrial estate in the industrial town of Yokohama, outside the Mazda research and development centre.

Maybe here we would discover how the Japanese make their cars so well. I'd already been to one of their car factories and could find no differences at all between their processes and ours.

We have robots. They have robots. We have line workers. They have line workers. They have big digital boards showing targets. We have big digital boards showing targets. And yet, when their cars roll into the sunshine, they don't break down. And ours do.

I've even asked Japanese people why this should be so and I genuinely believe they don't know. They simply can't work out why a car should ever go wrong.

I mean, a Japanese car made in Britain is more reliable than a European car made in Britain. Why?

And all I can assume is that errors are eliminated in the design stage; that the engineers spot potential problems before the car comes off the drawing board. Mazda's R&D centre might provide an answer.

The man sent from the reception area to welcome the 'respectful journalists of UK' had brought an umbrella but it was of limited use because he was nine inches tall and I'm 6 ft 5 in. Plus, I was standing up straight and he was bent double in the best bow I would see all week.

Now on my last visit to a Japanese car factory, the workers were lined up, standing to attention, as the intercom system played Johnny Mathis's 'When a Child is Born' – a good English song, said our guide.

But that was Daihatsu in the boom days and this was

Mazda, a company that was losing money hand over fist during a time when the boom was no more than a long-forgotten rumble. So there was no Johnny Mathis; just a plate of Thai green curry in the canteen.

And then we were shown into a bunker which looked like the inside of Pinewood when the James Bond team were in town. Every straight edge had yellow and black chevrons painted on it, there were banks of flashing lights and lots of men scuttling about with clipboards.

But instead of a laser which would destroy the planet, they were in charge of a machine that ran up and down some rollers and which had cost about the same as an air force.

Inside, you sit in what's supposed to be the driver's seat of a car, with pedals, a steering wheel and all the usual controls, but instead of a windscreen there was a screen which showed a computerised image of the road ahead.

Never mind that all the other traffic looked like it came from the creators of *Postman Pat* or that the road didn't appear to have any potholes or bumps. This was the world's most expensive driving simulator, installed so that Mazda's engineers could get a feel for what a car will be like without actually building or driving it.

Well I had a go and can report that when you accelerate, it tilts backwards and when you brake, it tilts forwards. It rocks from side to side too when you turn the wheel and I don't doubt that it's very, very clever. Certainly, I couldn't have designed it.

But then I also couldn't have designed the latest range of amusement-arcade machines which are faster and a damn sight more realistic.

If Mazda really thinks this helps get a feel for what cars are like on the open road, there's small wonder their cars are so unutterably dull. The only way to find out if a car is nice to drive is to get a real person to drive it on a real road, but this is not an option in Japan of course because all the roads are full.

They're probably a bit emptier in the countryside but your new car would be three years old before you got there.

However, while a machine like this will result in a dull car, it is interesting to note that if they're prepared to go this far in the design stage, I may well be right. Errors are hammered out of the equation on the drawing board.

And now, having mastered that trick, Japanese car firms are starting to design their cars outside Japan. If they can marry European and American flair with an ability to get things right, they will be unstoppable.

Honda didn't start making cars until 1966 but just 30 years down the line they have factories all over the globe and 90,000 employees. They use British chassis engineers, American stylists and Japanese engineers to create wonderful machines like the CRX, the NSX and the Prelude. Honda is more than a force to be reckoned with. It is The Force.

But I don't care. I still don't like Japan. The traffic back to Tokyo from Mazda's place was even worse than it was on our way out, but sitting on the expressway (ha ha ha), with the engine off, gave me a chance to take in some of the sights.

In a British traffic jam, drivers do things. They shift about in their seats, pick their noses, make calls, sing along to the radio. And it's the same story in Italy: people there do lots of things like getting out of the car and running round waving their arms about.

But in Japan, people in jams just sit there like they're made out of stone. I began to wonder how long they would need to be stationary before they blinked. Maybe they never would. Maybe they'd just sit there until they were dead. Maybe they were dead.

I was really staring at the guy alongside and there was plenty of evidence to support this theory . . . until I started to laugh at his car.

You see, in Tokyo you pay £200,000 for 3.3 square metres of living space, which means that even the super-rich have to endure truly dreadful living conditions in cramped, noisy, three-room flats that cost half a million or more. And you can't move out of town because you'd never get there, let alone back again.

Some people ship their families out and stay in city-centre hotels during the week, in rooms which are, in fact, 6-foot-long tubes. No kidding, you sleep in a pipe, pay hundreds a night and have to fork out even more for a toothbrush from the vending machines.

Everything in Japan comes from a vending machine. You could buy a sewing machine from a vending machine and more than once we found machines selling soiled panties, along with a photograph of the teenage girl who'd done the soiling – but at £5 a go, we usually managed to walk on by.

We were equally resilient to the appeal of a soft drink called Sweat.

Anyway, the point is: in a place like Tokyo, you can't really show off with your house, and so the only chance you get is out on the road . . . with your car.

Over half the cars there are white but very nearly 100 per cent are in some way customised. The car-accessory business in Japan is worth £10 billion a year and it's hardly surprising when you see the inside of a Japanese car-accessory shop. The air-fresheners department alone is bigger than Sheffield.

Then there's the steering-wheel section where you can, should you wish, spend two hundred quid on something in purple. They like purple over there, obviously.

This guy alongside me in the jam had gone for the purple steering wheel, but he hadn't stopped there. He had what appeared to be a selection of doilies on each of the four seats, the wiper blades were gold (well gold-ish), the exhaust pipe looked like the barrel of something from Matrix Churchill, there were extra lights and a sort of Fablon coating to make the windows opaque. It hadn't worked – I could see the vast range of air fresheners which were lined up on the dash.

Then there were his wheels. These were huge alloys which would have looked stupidly big on a Formula One car but which completely dominated his Nissan Cedric.

Here was one of the nastiest cars ever made, which had been made to look even worse by a man who obviously didn't know where to stop. That car really was a million pounds spent at Woolworth's.

But what made me laugh most of all was the words all over his wheels. In Japan, they find Western writing exotic, not the order of the words but the shape of the letters. They will buy anything if it has an English word on it, no matter what the word is.

Thus, the writing said, and I really do quote, 'Just a roller skate, grand touring, all over the physical ironic power'.

Here was a dead person driving the nastiest car in the world with gibberish written on each of the wheels. It was funny, right up to the moment when he came back to life, got out of his car and started banging on our windows. He was shouting a lot, and foaming slightly at the corners of his mouth, but I got the picture. He wanted to do pugilism or whatever the sumo equivalent is, and I must confess the temptation to get out and kick him in the fork was strong, but instead we locked the doors.

And continued to sit there, thanking God that we had not chosen to laugh at anyone in a black or dark-grey S-Class Mercedes-Benz.

These cars are driven by members of the Yakuza, a Japanese criminal organisation which seems to spend a lot of its time chopping people up. Sometimes, when there is no one to dismember, they'll chop themselves up.

Basically, they seem to run the seamier side of Tokyo – prostitution, gambling and so on – which is obviously lucrative because many of the senior members have paid for plastic surgery to make themselves look more evil. Their foreheads are lowered, their eyebrows are moved closer together and assorted scars are added as a sort of garnish.

They wear suits of a style not seen since Al Capone

went west, only the colours they choose are very nineties. Apple green is popular. So is sky blue.

They don't look when they cross the road either. I was chatting to one while strolling around looking for somewhere to do the televised interview, and when he wanted to cross the street, he just set off.

An inconvenienced car driver dared to blow his horn and my interviewee simply looked in the direction of his bodyguard and cocked his head at the hooter-blower's registration plate. The poor chap had to spend all that night trying to pick up his teeth with two broken arms.

If a Yakuza member upsets his seniors, he is forced to cut off a finger of his choosing. They're that brutal.

This is why you don't laugh at them in traffic jams, and also why Mercedes do not want them as customers. You see, if Mr Yakuza decides he doesn't want to pay for his car, he won't and there's not a lot Mr Merc salesman can do about it.

I heard stories about the Japanese underground movement, about how they made the Mafia look like the Brownies, but it wasn't until I actually met two of them that I believed it.

So here's a tip. If ever you're over there, you can ignore all the rules of the road but if ever you see a black Mercedes coming up behind, for God's sake get out of its way.

This, of course, is hard in Tokyo, because you can't really pull over anywhere. You certainly can't park.

All on-street parking was filled up in 1957 so newcomers must resort to multi-storey car parks, which have to be seen to be believed. You drive onto a turntable which spins your car round, so that it's pointing into what looks like a cave.

When you drive in, you find yourself on a ramp at the bottom of a lift shaft. A multitude of flashing lights signal that you have about six seconds to get out of the car, out of the building and, if you've any sense, on the next plane to somewhere else.

What happens when you're out is that the car is whisked away by what can only be described as a giant rotating vending machine. When you want it back, you put your money in the slot, punch in your code and your car is brought back to terra firma. Amazing.

And a damn sight better than risking it on the street. If you get it wrong, and it's easy in a country where you can't even understand the writing, you will be clamped, which involves having a yellow tag fastened to your wing mirror.

Astonishingly, the Japanese toddle off to the police station and pay to have it removed before driving off. Seriously, the shame of being seen with a yellow tag on your door mirror is enough of a deterrent. I told you it was odd over there.

If you've parked really seriously, a tow-truck takes your car to the other side of the city and traffic wardens write in chalk on the road where it is and how you can get it back. If it rains and the chalk gets washed away, tough.

This is how bored we'd become in our jam. We were actually talking about parking regulations.

But you can't be classed as truly bored until you move onto the subject of psychology.

Ten minutes later, I asked our chauffeur about Japanese psychology. Why don't they riot? Why don't they burn down parliament buildings? Surely, they could do a bit of raping and pillaging. I mean this place is a wart on the backside of the planet.

It seems the Japanese motorist lets off steam by joining the Midnight Club. These guys won't let you in unless your car can do at least 300 kph, but if you can prove that it does, you meet up at a service station, late at night when the roads are busy rather than jammed, and you race.

It's awesome: the Porsche 911 turbo has always been king of the hill but now the Nissan Skyline GTR has become a firm favourite. But don't think for a minute these are standard cars – they're not. One guy is reported to have spent a million quid hand-building a 911 which could do 354 kph.

But if you think these people are idiots, I can only assume you've never met a drifter. Mostly young, they're rich(ish) kids who, on a Saturday night, take their Nissan 200s along the intestinal road up Mount Tschuba. Fast. Very fast.

It's quite well organised so that beginners operate on the lower, less-demanding part of the road, intermediates are allowed halfway up and the experts are at the top.

The idea is that you drive along, trying to ensure that the rear wheels of the car are never in line with those at the front. You see how far you can go in an oversteer slide.

I have to tell you that some of them are very, very good, but when the car is on the ragged edge of its performance

envelope, things can go wrong, especially when you remember this is a public road that isn't closed. They say no
one has been killed, but then Japan also says it wasn't to
blame for the Second World War.

Strangely, the police don't ever go up the mountain, believing that if the kids are all there, they're not anywhere
else.

But they do stop cars which are obviously set up for
drifting, if they catch them out and about in Tokyo during
the week. A drifter's car, by the way, is noticeable by the
lack of a rear seat, which has been replaced with a selection
of spare wheels and tyres.

One young guy, if stopped by the police, simply says
that he is a welder who likes to practise on his own car.
And they believe him.

We managed to talk about the rights and wrongs of drifting for at least an hour, without turning a wheel. And then
we messed around with the in-car entertainment console
which lets you learn English and even plays blackjack.

Then we played 'I spy' but after 'c' and 'r' we were
stuck. We even listened to the radio but it was just like
the television, only without pictures. This is the only
country in the world that never seems to play any Phil
Collins hits.

Eventually – I think it was four days later – we were
getting nearer the hotel and I spotted an overhead gantry
with some lights. A new thing to talk about. We set about
it with vigour.

It seems that all of Tokyo's major routes are monitored
by cameras whose pictures are fed back to a central control

centre, which looks just like wartime bomber command. The people there pass this information about hold-ups to the motorist through the overhead gantries, each of which, I learned, is a giant map of Tokyo.

The idea is that when traffic slows to less than twenty or so on a particular road, it is depicted as an orange route. When traffic is stopped, it becomes red.

It's a fantastic idea this, but it doesn't work because every single road is red all the time.

The boards can even tell you how long it will take to get from wherever you are to various points around the city. We were a couple of miles from our hotel but that, according to our board, would take three hours. And it was bang-on right.

It even knew about the roadworks. Now, if there is one aspect of Japanese life that should be brought to Britain – and there is only one – it's their ability to fix a road.

You can forget all about miles of cones which have been erected to protect an upturned wheelbarrow. Over there, an army, the likes of which hasn't been seen since Iwo Jima, descends on the area and stands in serried ranks while the chief reads out instructions.

They are then dispatched and what we saw next defied belief. In five minutes, the afflicted section of road was cordoned off by a line of cones and a bank of lights that would have shamed Pink Floyd.

Men in reflective vests waved batons around to direct motorists, but these were no ordinary batons because you could write messages in the night sky with them. They were astonishing.

I was mesmerised for at least five minutes, by which time the army had done the road work and was taking the cones and the lights down. Ten minutes later, there was no evidence that they'd ever been there, that they'd staged a full-scale reconstruction of the closing scene from *Close Encounters*.

We talked about that all the way back to our hotel, where we arrived at a cool 10.00 p.m.

Ordinarily, we like to shoot four usable minutes of film in a day but in Japan, we'd managed about 30 seconds – half a minute of television for eight hours in a jam.

Another secret about *Motorworld*. The crew gets on well. We go out a lot in the evening and drink. We eat well. We have a good time. But in Japan, night after night, we finished work, went back to our rooms and went to sleep. I even had notches on my bed counting down to the day when we could leave.

We couldn't be bothered to go out because it was too much effort in a country that offers no rewards.

The car is finished there but that's only one of a hundred reasons why I shall never go back.

Switzerland

Your dinner party is a bit lacklustre and you've noticed the guests have started to glance at their watches, so simply lean forwards and ask this question: if you had to shoot just one person, who would it be? The next thing you know, they'll have drunk all your best port and, outside, the birds will be singing. And the debate will still be raging.

Mark Thatcher is always up there as a hot favourite but Jeffrey Archer is never far behind. More earnest people go for obscure Serbian leaders or Third World dictators and Tony Blair usually gets a mention too, from people on both sides of the political spectrum. I always go for Colin Welland, but can rarely find support on that one.

The game has become so prolonged that we've now introduced a new twist. Given a nuclear device, where would you set it off?

This isn't quite so successful because after just an hour, everyone is usually in full agreement. Japan always starts out as the obvious choice but they've had two already so it hardly seems fair to give them a third. Essex always provides some healthy debate too, as do France and Sydney, but it never takes long for someone to sit bolt upright and say 'Switzerland'.

That's followed by a pause as everyone weighs up the pros and cons and then, usually, everyone starts to nod.

Yes, Switzerland, and not only because this is the only country on earth where everyone has a fallout shelter under their stairs.

It's strange, this, because on paper, Switzerland has so much in its favour: breathtaking scenery, proper skiing, clean food, nice clocks and, to cap it all, we've never had a war with them. Well, they've never had a war with anyone, actually.

I think the big problem is jealousy. I mean, here we have a country with one of the highest standards of living in the world, a country with negligible unemployment and a country that's had the good sense thus far to stay out of the EC and which, as a result, has made its inhabitants rich beyond the dreams of avarice.

Here's a country with decent services, trains that run on time, bank accounts that are out of bounds to spying tax authorities, pretty lakes and a reputation for fair play. It's no accident that the Red Cross's emblem is a reverse of the Swiss flag.

It's a nice place but that's nothing to be proud of. I know lots of nice people; liberal, kind-hearted souls who help old ladies across the street and who never have a bad word for anyone. But without exception, they are dull. These are people who can put someone to sleep just by saying hello.

Their life is spent trying to arrange their facial expressions to match the moment, and they end up with no expression at all. And they're so desperate to avoid causing offence, they never say anything even remotely interesting either.

It's the same story with Switzerland. Britain has given the world jet engines, concentration camps, hovercrafts, television, skiing as a sport, telephones and football hooligans.

The Swiss haven't even got round to inventing their own language, preferring instead to butcher that most ridiculous of tongues – German.

The national pastime out there defies belief. Millions of them have taken to collecting the foil tops from UHT-milk cartons. You can see hundreds of full-grown men rummaging around in bins, looking for something unusual to add to their collections.

The shops are full of rarer examples which sell for seven quid a go and the personal ads in the back of newspapers are stuffed full of swapsies. This is for real. The rest of the world is on roller skates and the Swiss are at home, sticking milk-carton tops in photograph albums.

I first became aware of a problem back in the mid eighties when I found myself with an hour or two to kill at Zurich airport, which was closed because of snow. It's good to see, I thought, that even the most efficient country on earth can screw up sometimes.

And then I started to think more carefully about that efficiency as I strolled round the duty-free shops, smoking. Before I'd even lit the cigarette, I found myself being shadowed by a small man with an overall and a long-handled dustpan and brush. And each time I flicked the ash he was there, sweeping it up, keeping everything nice 'n' shiny.

A few years later, I was on a skiing holiday in Zermatt, trying to squeeze inside one of the ridiculous milk floats they call taxis. There was a sign saying it was a six-seater but there was no way my left leg, complete with its ski boot, would get inside and this infuriated the driver. The brochure had said it could seat six, and he was damn well going to get six people inside, so he set about my errant leg, kicking it until the door would shut.

This is not what you'd expect from a people whose country plays host to the Red Cross, UNICEF, the World Health Organisation, the Worldwide Fund for Nature, the World Council of Churches and 150 other outfits dedicated to saving lives, not kicking people and having large, flash offices on the shore of Lake Geneva.

But this is only one side to Switzerland. You must not lose sight of the fact that every single male aged between 20 and 42 must spend at least two weeks a year in the army. Some spend more and some, those who've been clever enough to lose a limb in a farming accident, are let off, but here we have a fighting force with 400,000 men.

Who get to keep their guns at home. Officially, there are two million licensed weapons in Switzerland but everyone knows the real figure is closer to eight million – not bad for a country that only has six million people.

Everyone also knows that Switzerland is where the world's terrorists come with a shopping list, and I know why. In my short stay, I was offered a brand-new Kalashnikov with a thousand rounds of ammunition for £300.

A thousand pounds would have secured the latest piece of laser-sighted hardware from America, or maybe a grenade launcher, complete with instructions on how to get it into Britain.

It is by no means uncommon in Switzerland to see someone walking through the woods with an AK47 slung over one shoulder, but interestingly, only 80 people died violently in 1994 – and a big chunk of those were suicides. The American gun lobby should use Switzerland as proof positive that guns don't kill people. People kill people.

And the Swiss will kill anyone who tries to take their country by force. Contrary to popular myth, they do have a navy which patrols the lakes, but there are less obvious signs, too. Look carefully at the entrance to various tunnels and you'll see camouflaged gun emplacements. Peer under some of the graceful motorway bridges and you'll notice they've been mined, ready to be blown up at a moment's notice.

There's more. The motorways have been designed to double up as makeshift runways in a time of war and you're never left in much doubt about the sort of air power Switzerland can muster.

Go hiking in the mountains and you'll find valleys full of warplanes waiting for the Germans to get bolshy again. And then there are level crossings for jets.

These look just like train-type level crossings but the barriers come down to let Mirage fighters take off. It seems that as planes have needed longer and longer runways, they've been extended irrespective of what was in the way.

But what are the Swiss so worried about, for heaven's sake? I mean, taking the place is a tactical nightmare thanks to all those mountains and what do you end up with if you win? Which you won't. Some meadows and a cuckoo-clock factory.

Hitler couldn't even be bothered, though it is said this was because all his wealth was stored there. He even joked about the place, saying that when his armies had conquered Europe, he would take Switzerland with the Berlin fire brigade.

This, of course, was not possible, because you are not allowed to take Switzerland with a fire brigade.

It's one of many, many things you are not allowed to do in Switzerland, like wash your car on a Sunday, or hang your washing outside or run over a pigeon.

This must be the only country in the world where they have a special sign which is made at great expense and hung up throughout city centres, advising passers-by that roller-skating is not allowed.

I could fill the rest of this chapter with rules that would curl your hair and straighten your pubes but instead, we'll just concentrate on what Switzerland is doing to make life a misery for the motorist.

In some places, like Zermatt, they have simply banned the car altogether and replaced it with a weird collection of electrically powered boxes on wheels. These sneak up and down the nauseatingly quiet main street, running over everyone who didn't hear them coming.

But don't worry. They can't go quickly because there are still speed bumps all over the place. Do worry, however, if you need an ambulance and they roll up with something from the set of *The Clangers* to take you to hospital.

You get the impression they'd like to ban cars all over

Switzerland but even the greenest politician out there knows this is not really on. So they've instigated a policy of gentle persuasion instead.

Ten years ago, they spent an absolute fortune widening roads and building huge intersections so that traffic could move smoothly and efficiently in a country that prides itself on such things.

But now they're digging up the new lanes and making the intersections deliberately complicated. In towns, they are letting people in mental hospitals design the one-way systems so that they are useless and parking spaces are being cut.

This would be enough to drive every motorist to despair but to rub it in, they have gone bus-lane crazy. In Geneva particularly, they've crammed cars into inch-wide slots on the boulevards and avenues, allowing buses and cyclists enough space to drive around sideways.

This is costing a fortune. Quite apart from the cost of digging up roads, and making new and ever more elaborate signs, they are pumping billions into the public transport network to make it more and more attractive.

But here's the thing. There are 1750 different banks in Switzerland, and all of them are run and staffed by fat bankers who have facial topiary and large Mercedes. And frankly, they are hardly likely to give up Strauss on the stereo and air conditioning in favour of a hot tram.

So they continue to drive to work, even though they don't understand the new road layout, can't park when they get there and will be fined thousands of francs should they be unfortunate enough to run over a pigeon.

The motorist in Switzerland is down on the ground with a broken nose and two cracked ribs but still the government stands over him in hobnailed boots shouting, 'Had enough, bastard? Had enough?'

Their latest game is to ban all noisy cars and motorbikes, which is no bad thing if the limits were set by sensible human beings. But in Switzerland, they're so draconian that the TVR Griffith is outlawed. Furthermore, cars with automatic gearboxes have to be two decibels quieter than those with manual shifters. No one knows why, and every car manufacturer I spoke to says the only way to achieve this is to make manual cars deliberately noisier.

Then there are the fines. Drive too fast and they'll take your house and sell your children into slavery. They really are quite open about this – the Swiss government is proud of its stand against the car.

And the Swiss people are right behind them. I know we're talking here about a people who will report their next-door neighbours for parking illegally, but when they had a referendum on the speeding issue they actually voted for lower limits on the motorway. Then they voted again for higher petrol prices.

This is not because they're sick, or congenitally deformed; it's because they're frightened.

In the 1930s, Europe was under the spell of fascism, which was defeated. In the 1960s, there was the ever-present threat of communism but once again, the horror has gone away.

But there will always be anti-establishment figures who want to bring down free thought and democracy. Idealism will never go away, it just surfaces every few years with a different corporate identity.

And in the 1990s it's back under the environmentalist banner. This time, though, the idealists are really on to something because in their quest to bring down commercialism and give power to the people, they have touched a raw nerve. If we carry on like this, the planet will die. In five minutes of geological time, we have turned paradise into a rubbish skip. The Dutch will drown.

And the Swiss have gone for it big time. In 1985, someone with a beard announced that the forests in Switzerland were dying and that drastic action was needed, right now, if the whole country wasn't to become Europe's first desert. He even gave the problem a worrying name – Wallestappen.

This terrified everyone: their green and lush country had cancer. The green movement got a toehold, which is all it ever needs to put a stranglehold on common-sense politics and lower speed limits were introduced, not for safety reasons but for the sake of the environment.

They even talked about an immediate overnight ban on all cars without catalytic converters. Well that's just great – a million cars off to the scrap heap, no compensation for the owners and the polluted air from factories in northern Italy and southern Germany still tumbling over the borders.

Today, there is more wooded area in Switzerland than there was ten years ago but, even so, surveys show that 70 per cent of Swiss people still think the forests are dying.

The forests, in fact, are fine. It's Switzerland's car enthusiasts who are dying. A recent count showed there are only seven left.

One is Franco Sbarro, whose factory and school is in the twee little lakeside town of Grandson. Here he teaches students from all over the world how to design cars, an art he practises down the road in his workshop.

This is a remarkable place because slung up in the rafters you'll find a couple of BMW MIs, several rare and exotic motorcycles and the odd GT40. And that's not all because one room is stuffed full of engines. He has a couple of 3.3 Porsche turbo units, a Ferrari V12 and even a Merlin from a WW2 Spitfire.

Customers simply pick an engine and Sbarro tosses a few styling ideas at them. Maybe sir would like a mid-engined Golf? Or perhaps a Fiat Cinquecento-type car with a Lamborghini 12-cylinder motor? Anything is possible.

I drove a car that had started out in life as a Ferrari Testarossa but which had been stripped of its original body and equipped with something truly outlandish in plastic. It had no windscreen, looked like it had just landed and had two huge tubes running down the flanks. These acted as rollover bars but also fed cool air from the front of the car into the mid-mounted engine.

Then there was the swimming-pool-blue car. This one had a Jaguar V12 engine mounted at the back, but that was all it shared in common with a normal car. It looked like something *U.F.O.*'s Commander Straker would dream about driving. It didn't really work though because it had a 75-foot turning circle and a steering system where the wheel was connected to the front wheels via a vast drum of yoghurt.

It was also not as fast as it should have been. Indeed, it was not as fast as a Metro but this, said Sbarro, was because it isn't finished. It was designed simply as a styling exercise, a car to turn heads and snap knicker elastic, something it did rather well. I got through three pairs in an hour.

It's odd to find such remarkable cars being made in Switzerland and I put this very point to Monsieur Sbarro, who answered quickly, 'Ah yes. But I am Italian. I just live here.'

It's just about the same story down the road at Rinspeed. This little outfit started out in life as a tuning workshop but has now moved into full-scale production with the aluminium-bodied Roadster.

It has a supercharged, 5.0-litre Ford Mustang V8 engine, rear tyres like lawn rollers and an interior that simply must have been designed by artist Roger Dean. To complete the picture, the test car I drove was bright orange.

Again, quite a surprise to find such a car being made in Switzerland. Er, well it isn't. It's actually built in America.

The last true Swiss car company was Monteverdi, which made some beautiful and very fast machines until the late seventies but these were styled in Italy, powered by Detroit engines and Monteverdi is a very unSwiss name, if you ask me.

The Swiss will tell you that many cars have been made there over the years but really, they can't have been serious ventures because I hadn't heard of one.

And anyway, we're talking here about a country where

there is no motorsport. When Pierre Levegh's Mercedes left the road at Le Mans in 1955, killing 88 spectators, the rest of the world mourned but Switzerland simply banned all forms of competitive track-based car racing. And because it's still in force today, the Swiss Touring Car Championship is staged in Germany and France.

The Swiss have lost their love for cars, but you can't say the same about their relationship with the motorcycle. Outside Japan, they have the highest two-wheeler ownership levels in the world, and we're not talking about miserable little mopeds either.

The streets are chock-full of chopped-down, beefed-up Harley-Davidsons and Yamaha V-Maxes, all of which are far too noisy to be legal. And yet this is deemed acceptable.

There is also the Ecomobile, a motorbike with an enclosed cabin and quadraphonic sound, that looks like a cross between a helicopter and an egg. It's a pretty groovy device this, with little stabiliser wheels that drop down when you stop, but it costs £50,000 which is a bit off-putting. Swiss labour rates are blamed and it's a shame because I rather liked it, in the same way that I find Kate Moss attractive. She isn't . . . but you know what I mean.

I will say though that there was something desperately clinical about it. It was a bike, but it wasn't, somehow. It was too high-tech, too clean and too functional for that. And it wasn't a car, either, because it didn't have enough wheels. It was neither here nor there.

And the same went for the Love Ride we encountered. This was a Sunday morning meet where a couple of thousand Hell's Angels tore around the countryside on their Harleys with Peter Fonda at the head of the column . . . raising money for charity.

There was something very unthreatening about the whole show. I spoke with a guy who hadn't washed his hair for twelve years, or cut it for six. He hadn't shaved in a month or bathed in a year and he was bedecked in leathers and filthy denims.

But he wasn't scary because on the back of his jacket it said, Hell's Angels – Swiss Chapter, and there is something very comfy, reassuring even, about anything with the word 'Swiss' in it. It's like beating someone to death with the *Mail on Sunday*.

Plus, instead of the goat's blood I expected to find in his glass, there was orange juice. Had he ever murdered a virgin or kicked someone's teeth in, I asked. 'No,' he said, 'but I have a fantastic collection of milk-carton tops. Would you like to see them?'

Mad, but what do you expect from a country that has declared war on the car, even though it failed to declare war on Hitler; a country that finds the AK47 acceptable but has outlawed the TVR Griffith.

This is not a place visitors can fathom easily. I suggest you don't even bother trying.

Vietnam

When we were choosing which countries to feature in *Motorworld*, there were important considerations. Would we get a suntan? Were the girls good-looking? How much was beer? If we were satisfied on these fronts, we'd ask whether there were enough motoring-related stories within the country, and whether each would back a central proposition.

In Italy, all the stories would be about passion. In Detroit, we had a social tale to tell. In India, we wanted to know why so many people were killed on the roads.

The tricky bit was making sure that the story each week was different. Having done four-wheel drive to death in Iceland other countries with lots of rugged terrain went out of the window.

The BBC executives understood this and nodded sagely whenever we discussed it. But why, they kept on asking, are you going to Vietnam? There aren't any cars there. It's communist. What if they think you're American? How the hell will you get there? What about visas? And, from the accounts department, 'How much is it going to cost?'

Frankly, my answers were rubbish. I put on my serious face and talked in long sentences, using the words 'whom' and 'synergy' a lot, but the real reason I wanted to go was much simpler.

A year earlier, while very drunk in a Wandsworth pasta restaurant, a friend who had emigrated to Saigon told me what happened in the city centre on a Sunday evening.

He explained that a thousand or more teenagers climbed onto their mopeds and rode round a preordained route. And he said they were all dolled up with no place to go because they don't have enough money. They had to ride past bars full of entrepreneurial big-nosed businessmen but they couldn't afford to stop for a beer.

They're poor beyond the ken of Western man and yet, he said, they all have mopeds.

It didn't make sense but I could see the visual impact of a thousand or more Vietnamese kids on mopeds cruising the sultry streets of Saigon all night long.

And coupled to the fact that Vietnam had just become the 49th country in the world to have a car industry, it was enough. Vietnam was going to be a *Motorworld* country.

Looking back, I would say that this was the second-best decision I ever made; the first being to take up smoking.

Before I went there, I'd always thought of Vietnam as somewhere that existed only to line the pockets of Hollywood fat cats. Vietnam was an excuse for Sylvester Stallone to cover his ample frame in mud. Vietnam was a war; not a country.

My only experience of Vietnamese people was either at a restaurant in Fulham or as a lot of scuttling midgets in straw hats throwing hand grenades into Huey helicopters.

In fact, this lot weren't really people at all, just a collection of Oriental extras on the big screen who got blown up for a living.

I didn't even know that 'Viet Cong' meant 'Communist Vietnamese' or that 'Charlie' was a nickname derived from the latter half of the VC radio call sign – Victor Charlie. The Americans had told me, endlessly, that they were simply a bunch of barbarians who made people play Russian roulette. And that, given half a chance, every six-year-old would put a land mine in my underpants.

The trouble is, of course, that since that last American helicopter heaved itself off the roof of the embassy there, we've heard an awful lot about 'Nam from the Yanks, but almost nothing at all from the country itself.

And this is hardly surprising. Here was a nation that had fought off the French, only to find that Sylvester Stallone was on his way. They'd beaten him too and that was it. They shut the doors on what they saw as a stupid, interfering world. And got on with their version of communism.

It was pretty tough by all accounts. Escaping boat people talked of a regime where coloured clothes were not allowed and motor vehicles were strictly outlawed. It made Moscow *circa* 1963 look like Surrey.

However, running a dictatorship is hard work and people usually tire of the effort, so after fifteen years the Government began to relax. Today, they're all on a day bed, sipping Pimms and having their feet massaged by half-naked Fijians. Vietnam is the most laid-back place on earth.

Sure, you can't set up in business there without a Vietnamese partner and every film crew has to be accompanied by two government minders, but these are not the sort of people who wear jackboots in bed and gaze longingly at your fingernails. We had a couple who looked like schoolteachers from Somerset.

The Americans have restored full diplomatic relations, the French are back, half the bars have exactly the same clientele as the White Horse in Fulham and the Koreans are building sixteen hotels a day.

In a few years' time, Saigon will look like a cross between Singapore and Bangkok. It will be horrid beyond words. But in 1994, it was heaven.

As a general rule, you should never judge a city, or especially a country, by the run from the airport to your downtown hotel. If you did that going from Heathrow to London, you'd think all England looked like Hounslow.

But in Vietnam, go right ahead, because our trip from the plane to the hotel was fabulous. There was an almost Mediterranean balminess to the place and the simple low-wattage streetlights only illuminated the nocturnal insect life in their immediate vicinity, so it was unusually dark too.

The daily thunderstorm had just finished erupting and the air was clear and still. The houses, for the most part, were in darkness too and only a few mopeds were out and about.

At this point, we'd been on the go for a while. We'd filmed for two weeks in Detroit, then flown for fourteen hours to Japan where we'd worked for another two weeks. It had been a brutal month, without a single day off, when we flew from Tokyo to Hong Kong, and then, after a four-hour stopover, on to Saigon.

Actually, it's called Ho Chi Minh City these days, but I was too tired for that sort of nonsense.

However, our driver kept us awake with a fantastic series of improbable manoeuvres that can only be described as breathtaking. He drove on whichever side of the road he saw fit and at crossroads, even when he didn't have the right of way, simply kept going. He reckoned that, as most people have mopeds, if there were to be an accident, we'd be fine.

Then there were the traffic lights – a graphic indication that Saigon is moving with the times. However, though they have been installed and are working, no one has explained to the locals that red means stop or that green means go. To our driver, and to all the other four million people in Saigon, they're just pretty lights on poles which have no meaning.

By the time we hit the Rex Hotel it was nearly midnight but we were wide awake. So we went to the Q Bar.

And then we went to a dive full of Australians called Apocalypse Now. And then the Caravelle. And then some place where we sat on the floor and another place where we fell on the floor. And then we started to wonder if it was worth going to bed because it was only an hour until we'd have to get up.

So we had a cyclo race instead. The cyclo is a bicycle at the back and an armchair at the front. You, the big nose, sit in the chair while Charlie sits on the saddle, pedalling you hither and thither. To go across town costs about three pence.

However, if you splash out, your chauffeur will pedal

faster which, of course, leads to a silent version of Formula One. The person with the most money wins the race.

There was something rather colonial about sitting there, cross-legged as a local pedalled as fast as he could to try and catch up with the cameraman. But it wasn't until we found ourselves going six abreast down Saigon's equivalent of Regent Street that I started to ask myself a big question.

What kind of a country is this?

If you can think of any other big city in the world where you could race in such a way, please let me know because, for damn sure, I've never been there.

Vietnam is relaxed because it hasn't really been exposed to the full horror of the Western tourist yet.

You are occasionally pestered by street urchins who are trying to sell godawful postcards and I was pickpocketed once. But even though sex is very openly for sale, don't be mistaken: this is not like anywhere else in Southeast Asia.

Because the Americans have been kept out for so long, there's no McDonald's, no pavement Coca-Cola dispensers and no one has been exposed to the violence of Hollywood. There are no gangs, and no one wears their baseball cap back to front.

You pay for everything with dollars but the government is trying to stop that. Under pressure from the idiots at the World Bank, steps are being taken to reintroduce the ridiculous dong.

This is a currency that makes the lira look sensible. To buy a street vendor's postcard, you need a shoebox full of the stuff. To buy an authentic wartime Zippo lighter, you'd need a Sherpa van to carry the cash. Oh, but don't be tempted, because on the bottom of a real Zippo you'll find it was made in Bradford, Pennsylvania.

On the bottom of the Vietnamese equivalent, which is scarred and battered to give that 'I've been through hell' look, it says, 'Rocky. Made in Japan.' Western tourists are stupid but I fear even Wilbur and Myrtle will see through this ruse.

They will, however, be impressed by the products of what was Vietnam's first car factory. Tucked away in a jungle ten miles from Saigon is a hut where 30 shoeless women and children sit in silence all day, chopping up beer and soda cans which are then bent and folded to become model helicopters, cars and trucks.

And they're brilliant. I have a Citroën Traction Avant which, in a former life, was a Heineken can. The cameraman paid the designer £5 to make a model of his camera. The guy was a genius but his biggest problem was a complete lack of artwork to copy.

When the producer gave him a dozen copies of *Top Gear Magazine*, stuffed full of pictures of Lamborghinis and Ferraris, he squeaked like a baby. I swear if we'd have given him a million pounds he'd have been less delighted.

But then again, when he gets some Seven-Up Diablos out on the streets, he'll have a damn sight more than a million I suppose.

Fired up with this success story, the Vietnamese government is now doing everything in its power to attract foreign car firms.

They have slapped a 200 per cent import duty on

all imported cars, which puts even the cheapest Korean hatchback way out of reach of just about everyone. A BMW 7 series is £50,000 in Britain but in Vietnam, you'd be asked for £200,000.

To get any sort of sales in Vietnam, car companies have to make their cars inside the country which creates jobs and, when exports start, brings in foreign cash.

And as a final twist, the car company can't do it alone. They must form a 50/50 partnership with a Vietnamese outfit.

But because Vietnam, everyone knows, is going to be the fastest-growing market in the world over the next few years, few motor makers are put off by the rules. Already, Fiat, Renault, Mitsubishi, Mazda and Daewoo are making cars and vans there.

But the biggest surprise of all is to be found at the bottom of a primeval backstreet in Hanoi. You pick your way through the foot-deep mud, dodging the oncoming oxen, to the factory gates, through which is a factory that is now making the BMW 5 series.

BMW sees Vietnam as the first country east of India where they can put one over Mercedes Benz. By making the car in situ, they'll be able to undercut Merc hugely, but this won't matter. One Vietnamese put it bluntly. 'We can't make cars. We wouldn't want to buy a car made here because we don't know how to do it. I want a Mercedes. Everyone here wants a Mercedes.'

It's the same story with their mopeds. You can buy a Thai-made Honda Dream for £2,000 but few do. Everyone is prepared to pay an extra thousand pounds because they want the real thing, the one that's made in Japan. And never mind that there is absolutely no difference whatsoever.

The moped has become a massive status symbol for the Vietnamese. It's their first, unsteady step up from the bicycle. It's the same as going home to your neo-Georgian house in England with a BMW.

Let me put the moped in perspective here. There are 10,000 cars in Vietnam. And six million mopeds.

Get up early in Saigon and you will not believe what the roads look like. It's a moving wall of Honda-ness.

They're coming at you down both sides of the road in an unending snake. Some are carrying an entire family – father, mother and three children – some have pigs slung over the handlebars, one chap we saw had a full-height wardrobe strapped to his back. But the danger biscuit was taken by an enterprising chap riding pillion while carrying an 8 foot by 5 foot mirror. It made my teeth itch with fear.

While standing on the pavement, it looks like a completely random, large-scale demonstration of Brownian motion. At a crossroads you have mopeds coming from all four directions but no one stops. Even though they now have the added distraction of pretty red, green and orange lights, four seemingly solid snakes just seem able to pass through one another.

The only reason I agreed to take part was because the speeds are low and the worst I could expect in a crash was a grazed elbow. Actually, the producer proved me wrong a few days later by coming off the back of the fixer's Lambretta and head-butting the kerb.

It was a remarkable injury, like someone had put one of his ears in a sardine tin key and simply peeled all the skin off his face.

But when I climbed aboard a Japanese-made Dream and set off, I hadn't witnessed a single incident. I felt safe. Confident. In control . . . even though this was the first time I'd ever attempted to ride any form of motorised two-wheeler on the public roads.

It took a while to eliminate the wobbling but, once mastered, I have to say driving in Vietnam was a piece of spring roll. From the pavement, you can't see the little signs from other riders, but they leap out at you like illuminated hoardings when you're in the thick of it.

At a junction, you know you're on a collision course with someone coming at you from the left but a little flick of his eyes lets you know exactly which way he intends to pass.

I guess I was a bit of a menace really, swerving to avoid manhole covers and making unexpected left turns, but as everyone in Vietnam was born on a bicycle and has been on two wheels ever since, they seem to have an innate, inbred sense of balance that would shame Barry Sheene. One day, there will be a Vietnamese world bike champion.

The best thing about Vietnam's love affair with the moped is that the traffic moves. There is no such thing as a traffic jam, even when two or three million people are trying to get into the city centre at seven o'clock every morning. This is a transport system without bus lanes, without a one-way system, without traffic-calming measures and it works.

There are buses though, which, like the trucks in Vietnam, are made out of old bedsprings and wood-burning stoves. And they're powered by the engines from old vacuum cleaners.

But you can't use them to commute. They're mostly for long-distance travel and are full, outside and in, of peasant farmers and all their year's produce. It takes two days to get from Saigon in the south to Hanoi in the north and you are expected to cook your own food on the move.

We'd been warned not to use internal air transport in Vietnam but, when we saw the alternative, we flung caution to the wind and flew everywhere. Mind you, when the pilot took three attempts to hit the runway at Hue, we began to wonder if two days on the bus wouldn't have been such a bad idea.

I mean, what's a bout of cholera between friends? You've never lived if you've never had a bit of heat exhaustion. And hey, it would have been a laugh being a human indicator for a while.

Yes, in Vietnam you can be an official, government-appointed human trafficator and it is your job to hang off the side of the bus, yelling at people. You don't actually indicate what the bus is going to do, of course, because you don't really know. You're just there to advertise its presence; that is, if you can make yourself heard above the drone of its 1950s vacuum-cleaner engine.

The other alternative to the moped is the taxi. But this, really, is not an alternative at all because it will break down.

The taxis in Vietnam all started out in life many, many

years ago as Chevrolets or Citroën Traction Avants. They had a hard life in the tropics and then, after the war, were squirreled away in hidey-holes for fifteen years.

Needless to say, they were not in good condition when private cars were allowed back on the roads, so the owners used ingenuity. I drove a Chevrolet whose engine, I'm damn sure, was from an air-conditioning unit. Also, it had no suspension at all.

But most of all, it had been equipped with bench seating for up to twenty passengers. This made the driving position a trifle cramped for a big nose like me; so cramped, in fact, that to get my foot on the clutch for a gear change I had to open the door.

It became a lot more comfortable after just a mile though because it jammed in second gear and stalled. Its owner wasn't in the least bit surprised and said he could replace the cogs with some fittings from a bedside lamp he'd found earlier in the week.

It is vital he keeps that car going because on his estate, he is king. It would be the same as peeping through your curtains and finding that your next-door neighbour had a Harrier GR7 jump-jet on his drive.

A car there, right now, is an impossible dream. But the moped is just within reach and that's why so many people spend so much of their disposable income, and a decent chunk of what is not disposable, on one.

Right now, in Vietnam, it is the only sensible means of getting around. And if it rains, which it does pretty well every day for half an hour or so, they just pull over and climb into their homemade polythene jump suits.

When it runs out of petrol, you do something even more strange. You see, Saigon is not yet high on the Esso hit list. There are no service stations with shops selling Staffordshire teapot and mint cake combos.

I was told that there are two garages but, in eighteen days, found neither.

It's not a problem though because every five yards down every street, you'll find a kid sitting there with what looks like a urine sample. It is, in fact, a bottle of petrol that he bought that morning, watered down that afternoon and is now offering to you for the tiniest mark-up. He can also fix punctures and would you like to meet his sister? She's very beautiful? Fresh?

You don't get that sort of service in a Shell Shop.

Time and time again, I was left in no doubt that Vietnam could teach the West a whole lot about civilisation.

Here is a country where anyone will do anything to help, at a price of course, but that's what makes capitalism tick. And then there's recycling. We applaud when BMW announces it has put reusable bumpers on its cars but, in Vietnam, nothing, and I mean nothing, is ever simply thrown away.

One farmer we met uses his one engine in his tractor six days a week and on market day, he transplants it to his van. At night, he uses it to power his house.

Then there's the cleanliness. Everybody's clothes are spotless. Everybody's hair shines so brightly you can't look, and they don't have Pantene Plus conditioner.

At night, you can pull over to one of a million families sleeping on the streets and buy a bowl of soup. It's a damn sight more nourishing than the *Big Issue* and the crockery squeaks with Nanette Newman freshness.

In fact, we ate local food from local restaurants most nights and there wasn't a single loose stool from anyone in eighteen days. More than that, if I had to say where I've had the best food in my life, I'd put the bus station in Saigon up there with the Pic in Valence.

Their spring rolls were like angels copulating on your tongue and then there was the 'rather burnt rice land slug' followed by 'carp soaked in fat'. The translation may have left a little to be desired but the food did not. It was exquisite, cost less than a pound and you didn't really mind after 23 bottles of Tiger beer that your table was sandwiched between two buses.

I simply adored Vietnam.

And you will too, when you go there on a package holiday in a few years' time. You'll love the brand-new hotel they've built, and the ice-white beaches. You'll adore the weather and the local cuisine, prepared by an imported German chef, will leave you speechless.

The traffic jams in the towns will be a bit of a bore though.

Yes, Vietnam will be a fully paid-up member of the twentieth century, but the world will have lost one of its jewels.

Australia

For a country whose most notable contribution to the world of television is a programme called *Neighbours*, it comes as quite a surprise to find the nearest big city to Perth is Jakarta. But don't expect a rugged, hairy-bottomed sort of town. Think more in terms of Milton Keynes and you're about there. Interesting motoring stories? Er . . . no. Not really.

Okay, so what about Sydney, likened by many to San Francisco? Oh come on. San Francisco is the best city in the world, with fine vistas, extraordinary hills, the Golden Gate, wonderful restaurants and an endearing blend of character and cleanliness.

Sydney is a huge, soulless sprawl where the people are chippy and the architecture is reminiscent of Birmingham. Except that Sydney doesn't have the International Conference Centre.

Again, if you attempted to make a motoring programme there, it would last about three minutes. 'Er, everyone drives Toyota Starlets.' The end.

I went to Queensland, too, where the coastline was tropical and unspoiled, but apart from a tendency to drive on the beaches of the Whitsunday Islands, I was still stuck. Cairns had nothing. Nor did Townsville. Australia was turning out to be a dead duck. Until I headed inland.

Peel away Australia's coastline and you're left with an area which is about the same size as America. And yet it has the same population as Leeds.

In outback Australia there is one person for every square mile and, to put that in perspective, in the Scottish Highlands there are twenty people for every square mile. Australia is enormous. And almost completely deserted.

Out here is where we would find the real Aussie action. Out here we could pose the question: what good is a car when your nearest neighbour is 300 miles away and there are no roads?

It's not as though we're talking about an arid desert. There are trees and, just below the surface, there are vast reservoirs of water which fell as rain three million years ago in Malaysia.

Obviously, the soil doesn't provide lush green Anchorbutter-type grass, but it isn't useless dust either.

This means that, every so often, you come across a farm which is so large it is rather hard for a European to get his head round the numbers. We needed to visit one, to find out about life in such remoteness, but were told, time and again, to get lost, in that polite way Australians have developed. 'Fuck off you Pommy bastard.' Something like that anyway.

Thick-skinned perseverance eventually saw us arriving at the truly enormous Wave Hill Station which is near . . . nowhere really.

It covers 13,000 square kilometres, making it the same size as Cornwall, Devon, Avon, Somerset and Dorset.

At any one time, 40,000 cattle are grazing on its

paddocks, but even so it's not the largest farm; not by a long way.

It isn't the most remote settlement either, even though the nearest shop is 280 miles away. The nearest pub is a 100-mile trek and to get to the nearest biggish town by road takes eighteen hours.

To get there, we flew for four hours from Perth to Alice Springs, during which time the view from the window was an unending sea of nothingness.

Then we climbed aboard a chartered eight-seater twin-prop aircraft for another four-hour flight over another sea of brownness to Wave Hill.

Actually, that's not quite true. We had to stop for fuel at a weird little airstrip which, quite literally, was in the middle of nowhere. And yet, in the departure hut, women in brightly coloured, floral-print dresses from the fifties were waiting for their bus to take them into town. A 'bus' in Oz is almost always a plane.

Our pilot refuelled on his own, switched the landing lights on by himself and took off with no clearance from air traffic control. There wasn't any.

And two hours later we touched down on the Wave Hill landing strip. All the farms out there have such things because cars are useless. In the Wave Hill garage there was a plane and anyone who drops by does so literally, from the sky.

If they need a doctor, he comes by air. Schooling for the two children is done over the radio airwaves but if they ever need to get to a football match, it must be done by Cessna.

There are cars on the farm but they're used for workmanlike things such as checking on bore holes and mending fences. Mind you, to get round all the watering holes is a three-day job.

And a damn dangerous one, too, because in the height of summer the temperature almost never goes below 120°F. When we flew in, it was 140°F, even in the evening, and that means it was hot enough to boil a tortoise.

Certainly, you don't need charcoal and firelighters for a barbecue out there. Drop a rasher of bacon on the ground and in a flash, you have breakfast.

It sounds like a hoot but if, while you're there, your car breaks down, you have 30 hours and then the eagles will be looking for the napkins.

Before you set off on a cross-country Australian drive, motorists are told to ensure that someone knows when you're supposed to arrive. And that no matter what, if you break down, you stay with the car.

It's all a bit of a fag to be honest, which is why everyone we met on our month-long tour of the outback had a four-wheel-drive Toyota Land Cruiser.

Until the end of the sixties, Land Rover had a 90 per cent market share and people took the endless mechanical maladies for granted. But then along came Toyota with a vehicle which just kept on going. It wasn't as stylish but no one was looking anyway.

In the very early pioneering days, people only ventured into the outback if they had the toughest vehicle money could buy. Most opted for a Rolls-Royce, not because of the prestige or that flying lady but because it was less likely to break down than a Model T.

The Australians went mad for the Land Cruiser and in just twenty years, Land Rover's market share was down to 2 per cent. They had been wiped out, along with most other British memories too. The pound became the dollar and the mile became a kilometre.

Wave Hill manager Gavin Hoad explained that he would never switch from Toyota. 'They're pretty reliable and we've had them long enough to know what will go wrong and when. That way we can keep the right spares here.'

Well they'd have to because the nearest Toyota dealership is a cool 280 miles away on roads which are basically dirt tracks.

In the Northern Territories there are no speed limits but don't get excited because realistically, 60 mph is your top whack.

First of all, there is the wildlife to worry about. A small kangaroo is no big deal – they just burst when you plough into them – and you needn't worry about emus either. But the eagles, they're a big problem.

Say there are twenty vehicles on one 300-mile stretch of road and in one night, they kill twenty animals each. That's fairly realistic. This means that as dawn breaks there will be 400 fresh carcasses in the ditch.

So the eagles come down and gorge themselves stupid. And just as they're enjoying the coffee and mints, you come bumbling along. Mr Eagle is scared and needs to take off but he's so full he has to face into the wind, which may well be the direction from which you're coming . . . at 60 mph.

It is by no means uncommon for the giant bird with its ten-foot wingspan to be at windscreen height when you collide. Thank you. And goodnight.

The eagles, however, are less of a danger than the road trains. These gigantic trucks can tow three articulated trailers at speeds of up to 100 mph thanks to engines which just defy belief. Each cylinder is 3.1 litres and for that little bit extra, a turbo is fitted as well.

The unit is 150 feet long. It does one mile to the gallon. If you were to fill it up in England, it would cost £1,000. Its stopping distance is measured in light years, and that's only if the driver bothers to hit the brake pedal.

The problem is simple. There are no tachographs in these huge trucks so there's nothing to stop the free-lance operators doing a thousand miles without a proper break.

To keep awake, and to make the deadlines, many use speed – the drug, that is. Some are so stoned they can have an accident and not even know.

Others thunder along while reading a book. If the wheel gets a bit wobbly in their hands, they know they've strayed off the road. Some use speed *and* read.

So, if you see a road train coming towards you, it's best to pull off the road. Right off it. Fifteen miles is the minimum safe distance.

It's worse if you come up behind one though, because on some roads the rear trailer can sway by as much as fifteen feet. And with sixteen axles, you can't begin to imagine how big the dust cloud is. We're talking here about a nuclear explosion on wheels.

The only way to go past is to keep your fingers crossed, hoping that the rear trailer is swinging the right way and that there's nothing coming from the opposite direction. There usually isn't, of course, because oncoming traffic is safely moored up fifteen miles from the road. Usually. But not always.

Small wonder most people fly everywhere. They even take to the air when they need to muster cattle.

Now in the course of making this series I've been in some spectacular and dangerous situations, but none even gets close to the hour I spent with Fox, a heli-musterer and certifiable lunatic.

Here's a fact. To fly any helicopter, and especially a Robinson R-22, you need both hands. And yet Fox could whizz along at 100 mph, six feet up, while rolling a cigarette. He could even light it – not easy as the doors had been removed and it was a bit draughty in there.

It was somewhere between awe-inspiring and terrifying before we saw any cows. But afterwards, all hell broke loose. Fox engaged what can only be described as 'plummet mode' and we simply fell out of the sky to a height of three inches.

In the process, the dashboard had lit itself up like Regent Street on Christmas Eve. Warning buzzers were drowning out the rotors and a massive red light in front of me warned 'low rpm'.

Whoa. Now we were going backwards and wait, what's this? A spin turn in reverse. New lights were coming on. New buzzers were joining in.

We were working in tandem with another helicopter

and two trail bikes. Well, 'tandem' is probably the wrong word because there didn't appear to be any coordination at all.

It was surprising, therefore, to note that after a minute or so, a giant herd of maybe a thousand cows was heading at full speed for the pens. Whenever the stampeding mass passed close to more cows, they'd join in, and if they didn't, we'd simply dart down to encourage them a bit.

One cow, though, was not going to play. He'd found a Michelin three-rosette piece of grass and he wasn't going to budge. He held his ground until the very moment when our helicopter's skids landed on his back . . . and began to push.

As soon as he did the decent thing, we had reversed into the ionosphere in a lurid spiralling move that very nearly resulted in a breakfastular explosion.

To take my mind off it, I engaged the intercom button and told Fox that the Robinson has a poor reputation for safety in Britain. He mumbled something about not losing too many each year and turned off the engine.

We were now in 'super plummet mode' and I was scared like I've never known scared before. The ground was coming at us like we'd pressed the hyperspace button and then we hit, the rear tips of the skids first and then the front.

We slithered along the ground for a while, by which time Fox had the Porsche engine restarted. And we took off. 'No worries,' he said.

Apart from the mess in my pants, I guess he was right.

Now I have a deep-seated fondness for helicopters,

and it was patently obvious that the heli–musterers knew exactly what they were doing. The camel musterers of Alice Springs, on the other hand, did not.

Camel is now a fairly regular main course in some of the more fun-filled Aussie eateries, but you can't just wander round the bush shooting them.

Here's why. There are more camels in Australia than there are in the Middle East and a booming export trade is the result. There are a few quid to be made but everyone in the business is hoping one day to catch a fast one. In Saudi Arabia, top racing camels fetch up to $8 million.

Primed, we arrived at a 10,000 square-kilometre farm out towards Ayers Rock where our hosts turned out to be a bunch of men who, at the age of seven, had walked into a hospital and had their brains amputated.

They'd invited us down for the hunt, saying we could stay at the Million Stars Motel, which turned out to be a patch of grass by their chow house. Crawling into my sleeping bag was like doing a lucky dip where the first prize was life. Just what was in there? A snake? A funnel-web spider?

It was a poor night's sleep for several reasons, chief among which was the enormous thunderstorm which passed by at 2.00 a.m. Then there was the ever-present threat of creepy-crawlies treating my nose as a light snack. And every rustle in the bushes was a large and fierce animal that scientists had believed, until that night, was extinct.

I spent most of the time shining my torch into the void until at 5.00 a.m. we were up, eating beans and clambering aboard a wide variety of seriously knackered old Toyota off-roaders. One towed a trailer full of spare wheels. 'On a bad day, we can use maybe 40 tyres,' said Gun, Denmark's only camel-catcher.

'We have Michael Palin coming here next month,' he added. 'Do you think he'd mind if we picked him up from the airport dressed as Gumby?'

Probably.

And off we went in search of camels who, it is said, have the intelligence of a nine-year-old child. Like hunting in Britain, therefore, the prey is brighter than the pursuer.

A lot brighter, because at 2.00 p.m. we'd seen diddly squat; no tracks, no shit, nothing. Motorcycle outriders had been to the top of every hill for a better view and each time they'd come back to say we were at the epicentre of a completely camel-free zone.

Except once. After half an hour of waiting, one outrider hadn't come back and we were concerned. His Australian colleagues didn't care less, though. 'What if he's injured?' I asked.

'He'll crawl home,' came the reply.

'But what if he's dead?' I went on.

'Well then it doesn't matter.'

The conversation dried up because, 200 yards in front, Mr and Mrs Camel had wandered out of the bush with their three children, Janet, Wayne and Paul. And the chase was on.

I made the mistake of leaping into the back of the lead vehicle, a Toyota pickup truck which took off into the scrub at, oh, about 80 or so.

Wherever the camels went, we had to follow and this was a big problem for little old me in the back. I had to stand up, holding on to the rollover bar, which, under the tropical sun, had become hot enough to fry an egg. Within twenty seconds my hands had become fountains. There was blood everywhere.

Then there was the ride, which was bad enough for the first mile when all four tyres were intact, but over the next six miles each one burst. To absorb the bumps, I had to keep my knees bent, which is fine for a few seconds in a stationary room, but in the back of a bucking off-roader which had no tyres, for two hours, it was intolerable.

Worse, though, were the trees. Regularly, our driver headed under a bough which, if I'd been looking the other way, would have taken my head clean off. This was abject misery.

When we finally caught up with the camel, Gun leaped off the Toyota, attached himself to its neck, and wrestled it to the ground. It was barbaric and when I asked why they don't just use tranquilliser darts, I was told 'Where's the fun in that?'

And all we had to show when the chase was over was a manky little bull worth about three quid and half-a-dozen shagged Toyotas.

Which kind of answered my original question. What good is a car in outback Australia? Well for catching camels, it's vital. And for doing bits and bobs round the ranch, it's essential.

But as a means of transport, as a device for getting from A to B, it's no good at all. I was going to say that outback

Australia is the only part of the civilised world where the car doesn't work. Distance defeats it. But I've just thought of something. Outback Australia isn't civilised.

Texas

The plane began its descent into Houston's international airport and I peered out of the window for my first-ever look at the Lone Star State – Texas. Land of the Free. Home of the Brave.

Oh deary me, I thought, I'm on the wrong jet. The pilot's gone mad. We've been flying around in circles for eleven hours. That's not Texas. That's Lincolnshire.

For as far as the eye could see – and from 15,000 feet on a crystal-clear day, that's a very long way indeed – it was flat, unrelenting and dull beyond even the ken of a party political broadcast speech-writer.

In the next two weeks, I would crisscross what is America's second-largest state looking for some geological eccentricity, but apart from a miserable little canyon up near Lubbock, there was nothing.

I'm told it's a bit deserty over by El Paso in the west but elsewhere it's a series of completely flat fields broken only, and very occasionally, by the odd corn thingy.

The towns, too, are unremarkable. God only knows what Tony Christie was thinking about when he immortalised the hateful sprawl that is Amarillo. There aren't even any decent titty bars.

And the most interesting thing we found in Lubbock was the airport car-rental desk. This is the town that gave the world Buddy Holly and James Dean. But both of them left.

So what of Houston? Well, it's no better I'm afraid. The skyline, built with oil money I suppose, is impressive in a pointy-type way, but the streets are almost completely devoid of human life.

For our first three nights there we walked the sidewalks at night, looking for bars and restaurants. We wanted action but all we got was a joint whose USP was an owner who encouraged us to throw the pistachio nutshells on the floor.

This is the fourth-biggest city in America. Home of NASA. Epicentre of the world's breast-implant industry. And, in 1994, provider of more than half the *Playboy* centrefolds.

And there we were in an awful little bar with Ry Cooder doing his best to slide some atmosphere into the joint by giving it some soulfulness on the geetarr.

It wasn't until the fourth day that we figured it out. All of Houston's shops, bars and restaurants are underground, linked by a series of walkways that would defeat Ranulph Fiennes. There were people down there who had voted for Lincoln.

It seems that Houston is a hot place – they've obviously never been to the middle of Australia – so to keep the shoppers happy, everything is tucked away below ground in air-conditioned splendour.

I hated it, and I hated our hotel which was where everyone in America had arrived for a bridge tournament. I hate bridge too.

But then, as is the way with our *Motorworld* forays to the edges of extremes, we started to meet the people. And a smile started to pucker the corners of my mouth.

First, there was Clyde Puckett, whose pickup truck had just been recognised, officially, as the ugliest in the whole state.

If he were to walk into your house, you would call the police first and the council health inspectors shortly thereafter. He was big, for a kickoff, and to complete the picture he had long hair tied into a pony tail and a beard whose most far-flung extremities reached down to his oft-exposed navel.

But here was a gentleman; a man of God who lived the simple life, way out in the hinterland with nothing but his truck and a dog – it was hard to tell them apart sometimes – for company.

We were there because I wanted to know why Americans in general, and Texans in particular, buy so many pickup trucks.

In order to be tough, and not to tip up when their rear ends are loaded down with 'stuff' – you hear that word all the time in Texas – they are burdened with suspension that would be more at home propping up a skyscraper.

Just walk up to a big Yankee pickup and try to make it rock. You might as well try to push the Tower of London over.

This means, of course, that if you hit a small pebble while driving a pickup, your spine will shatter. Your teeth will implode too as the vehicle rears up like an angry beast,

Italians have a fascination with machinery, they love the way cars are made. So, of the five supercar manufacturers in the world, three are in one Italian town – Modena.

Che Guevara looks down on the desolation that his revolution helped to create. Communism and cars go together about as well as haddock and ice hockey.

Detroit today, no longer car capital of the world ... more like the crime capital. Look at the sign in this car park – tailor-made to make you feel insecure and unwanted.

It's the most beautiful terrain on earth, but to get there you need specialised machinery, satellite navigation and a guide. And a snowmobile. And a hat. And some soup.

During our two-week stay in Tokyo, we didn't go out after work once. Had we attempted to do so, we'd still be there now. The traffic jams just have to be seen to be believed.

What is wrong with this picture? In Switzerland, there are said to be eight million guns in the hands of the six million population. Kalashnikovs are fine and can be bought for about £300. Grenade launchers are acceptable too — and they're even less. But the TVR Griffith is too loud, so it had been banned.

Cheesy. Not my grin. The man. Cheesy was one of those people who could put a smile on anyone's face. In the villages, he chugs along on his vintage motorcycle and sidecar combo but, on the open road, he prefers the thrill of two-wheeled motoring so we rode along like this for, oh, about twenty miles. If he's caught, he faces life imprisonment.

Now then. The Western world can do you all sorts of spectacular cars but none is quite so refined or quiet as the Vietnamese cyclo – a sort of bicycle-armchair combo that's yours for a day for about 10p (including driver). Give him 20p and you get there twice as quickly.

The sheer enormity and emptiness of outback Australia boggles the European mind. If this picture had been taken 100 miles further down the road, it would still have looked exactly the same.

Clyde Puckett. Crazy name. Crazy guy. Really crazy truck. It's just been voted the ugliest pickup in all of Texas but, even if Clyde wins the state lottery, he won't sell it. 'I'd fit power steering and some new tyres,' he said. But not air conditioning? 'Texas heat's good for you. It makes you sweat. Cleans the pores.'

You may think that making *Motorworld* was one long orgy of fast cars, loose women, supersonic boats and high living. But you'd be forgetting the expense account, candle-lit dinners, the sun-kissed beaches and the five-star hotels.

The buses are a hang-over from the British days but so too, sadly, is the bureaucracy which snarls every-thing up. There has never been an Indian Grand Prix driver. And, in all probability, there never will be.

The F-15 Eagle: f'in' fast.

before crashing down again with great vengeance and furious anger.

Of course, while it is up in the air, the wheels will not be on the ground, so you'll have no steering. But that's OK because thanks to your snapped back, you'll have lost the ability to turn the wheel anyhow.

The pickup truck is even more uncomfortable than a horse.

So let's look at the practicality. Well for sure, there's a great deal of space in the back for . . . um, it's hard to say what really. I mean, once in a while, maybe, you need to take an old sofa to the skip, but would you be prepared to put up with the bone-breaking discomfort on the other 364 days in a year? Certainly, in England we would not.

Especially as the huge rear end means there's precious little space up front for people. Most are capable of accommodating three alongside one another and some of the bigger versions have elongated cabs to provide space for five – but frankly, bearing in mind the average size of an American, we're talking two-seaters here.

To move this vast vehicle around, obviously, an equally enormous engine is required and that's why even the cheapest, most bland and plain models come with 5.0-litre V8s.

These, though, are usually tuned for torque, so that should you wish to spend your days uprooting giant redwoods, you'll be well equipped. Unfortunately the downside is no power.

When they're burdened with an automatic gearbox – and nearly all of them are because manuals in the States are as rare as non-remote-controlled TV sets – you would not believe how slowly they go.

People will tell you they have a 'lot of pickup', meaning they can get away from the lights quickly, but that's nonsense. An Escort diesel would leave even the most potent US doubly for dead.

And when it comes to top speed, forget it. The pickup truck doesn't have one. And nor would your car if it had the aerodynamic properties of a wardrobe.

Needless to say, they chew fuel too, which is just one more small reason in a sea of big ones to give the very idea of a pickup truck the sort of berth you'd give a bear whose cubs you'd just trodden on.

Explain this one then. In Texas in 1994, 21,000 people bought a Ford Taurus, which is the bestselling car in America. It's a sort of cross between a Mondeo and a Granada, but that's not really important just now. Remember the sales figure – 21,000.

In the very same period, 110,000 Texans bought a Ford pickup truck. In Texas, pickup trucks outsell cars five to one. The people there are very obviously as mad as it's possible to be without being incarcerated somewhere.

Clyde Puckett was not mad. He had a truck because he hauls 'stuff' for people . . . but he was the only one.

Down at the Broken Spoke 'dancing and dining' Bar, the car park was chock-full of pickups which, very obviously, had never hauled anything more arduous than the odd six-pack.

Inside, the customers told us that pickup trucks are safer, more convenient, more practical and better-looking than a car. But it's more than that. A truck is as much a part of the Texan uniform as a ten-gallon hat.

Suitably equipped with an electric-blue Ford F150, I headed out to meet a few more of these strangely daft people.

And happened upon Bill Clement. Bill runs a sort of Battersea Dogs Home for knackered Chevvies, picking out the best and restoring them. He has many, some of which he sells, and some of which live in his warehouse.

Dull so far, until he tells you that his favourite models are those which bear the high-performance SS insignia. 'They were not too popular among non-Third Reich enthusiasts,' he says, while sitting at his desk playing with a German helmet from WW2.

His desk, in actual fact, is the front end of a 1955 Chevvy but I was a little more bothered about the list of 'nigger names' he'd just plunged into my sweaty paw. 'What's your daughter called?' he barked.

'Er . . . Emily,' I stuttered.

'Nice name,' he said. 'Means something, unlike any of the names you'll find on that list.'

'What does Emily mean?' I asked.

'Oh, stuff,' he replied.

Getting to see Bill hadn't been especially easy as a large sign above his door made it perfectly plain who was welcome and who was not.

It went something like this: 'No bargain hunters, bleeding hearts, bullshitters, credit, cheques, computers, collegiates, deadbeats, drunks, daydreamers, non-Chevvy drivers, estimates, Fords, girlfriends, honking, metric,

politicians, peddlers, refunds, solicitors, sympathy, vaca-
tioners, wives or whiners.'

Things he liked included profanity, chauvinism, bitch-
ing, cash, impatience, bad attitudes, NRA members,
sloppy appearance and bigotry. Another sign on the
office window advised visitors to 'speak English or get the
fuck out'.

I was allowed in even though I was considered a 'crapass
limey', from the same country as the 'godawful' Rolling
Stones and the 'gall bladder of rock and roll' John Lennon.

I tried to show an interest in his impressive collection
of cars but his assistant, Bob, was much, much more
absorbing.

Bob was a large man who had bought a pair of jeans
when he was not quite so large. However, rather than diet
or throw them away, he had simply done them up under
his arse, letting his shirt tails protect his modesty.

That was fine until he bent over. It was quite a sight,
Bob's butt. It's a *Motorworld* moment.

Bill was talking. Did I want to take a drive in his
stunningly restored El Camino SS, a 7.4-litre 430-bhp
machine that was actually built at GM's Arlington plant
in Texas?

Well not if Bob's been driving it, I thought, but voicing
such a thought seemed rude, so off I went. 'Just don't
take it through Niggertown,' called Bill, usefully, as I
roared off.

It was a great car – well pickup actually – with exhausts
that sounded better than any Fender Strat. It didn't handle
and looked like it was on a day-release from the seventies

but I adored the pre-political correctness turn of speed. As Bill's T-shirt said, 'If you haven't seen God, you're not going fast enough.'

When I took it back, I asked if Bill was worried about his cars being stolen. 'No sir,' came the reply. 'If a nigger tries to come in here, we have the right in Texas to vigorously defend our property, up to and including killing him.

'I found a nigger trying to break in here once. He got an overdose of lead that night.'

'You killed him?' I asked.

'Sure did,' came the reply. 'Ain't no loss to society.'

The man was a social time bomb, a point that was proved as we interviewed him on camera. It took ten takes before we got a sentence without the words 'nigger' or 'fuck' in it.

My word, we thought, as we left. What an unusual person. Oh, how wrong we were. In Texas, Bill's a korma in a sea of vindaloo.

Take Stanley Marsh. Stanley is the boss of a TV station and, despite the sartorial elegance of a tramp, a respected figure in the local community.

He drives a pink Cadillac and spends his time dreaming up curious slogans for a series of road signs that you'll find all over his home town. You arrive at a crossroads and there, instead of a 'give way' sign, will be the familiar, authentic-looking diamond shape bearing the legend, 'Two-headed Baby' or 'Hear the Fat Lady Sing'. Odd, but not much use if you want to know the way somewhere.

Stanley's house was full of university drop-out types,

one of whom had modelled himself on Bob from Lubbock.
He wore his trousers so low down that you could see the
top of his penis. I don't know why but I kept wondering
if Douglas Hurd would ever do that.

I was still wondering when Dennis, our rather thought-
ful director, summoned up every ounce of energy from
his politeness genes and said to Stanley, 'Sir, I think it
would probably be a good idea if you were to drive . . .'

Dennis was shut down by a huge shriek from Stanley.
'WHAT IN THE HELL DO YOU MEAN,
"PROBABLY"? IF YOU WANT ME TO
DO SOMETHING, COME OUT WITH IT
STRAIGHT, BOY.'

No one has ever talked to Dennis like this, and at 51
years old, it's a long time since anyone called him 'boy'.

It seems that Stanley likes straight talking. He doesn't
mind being told to do something so long as it's in plain
English.

Plain English is a Stanley speciality. When I asked him
if there were more eccentrics in Texas than anywhere else,
he was off. 'No. I'd say there were a higher percentage of
dull people living around fish, living on islands.'

Was he, perchance, talking here about Britain?

'I sure am boy. I don't know how you can live on that
stupid little island. It smells of fish and is covered with
scales.'

Turns out that Stanley's no great limey fan, and he can
prove our uselessness when you get him onto the subject
of Stonehenge.

You see, up by the interstate near his house – called Toad

Hall – he has partially buried ten Cadillacs, nose-down, in a field. Why, I asked him, did you do such a thing?

'I wanted to build something better than Stonehenge,' came the reply. 'Took about a week.'

He now has a thing for burying cars so that on his immaculate lawn at home a bright orange VW Beetle is buried up to its windscreen. Crazy guy. No he really was. He's the only Texan we met who didn't have a pickup truck.

I was in a state of despair about Texas until we arrived in Austin, which is the state capital. You know that because the government buildings are an exact replica of the White House, only in true Texas style the dome is slightly larger.

I knew I would like this place when we were told that the only statue in town was there to honour Stevie Ray Vaughn, the local boy who became a guitar legend.

Music is the thing here. Walk down 6th, any time of day or night, and you will hear everything from the blues to C and W to old time rock and roll. Every building is a bar and every bar has a live band. Forget Duval in Key West. This is it.

Strangely, for America, the road is pedestrianised and the only vehicles allowed are horse-drawn. People have to park elsewhere and walk – a word you don't hear too much anywhere in the US.

I did a lot of 'walking' around the back streets and couldn't believe what I was seeing – no pickups. Well, there were a few round the back of Country bars, but everywhere else the parking zones were filled with Hondas and Toyotas and little Dodges.

It turns out that Austin has the largest university in America with more than 50,000 pupils from all over the States. That gives it a cosmopolitan feel. I liked it because for two glorious days I forgot I was in Texas.

Eventually though, it was time to leave because back in Houston we had our biggest-ever *Motorworld* interview. We had been granted an audience with all three members of ZZ Top.

This had taken months of preparatory work, even down to a discussion with their manager about Dusty's perspiration problem. It was explained to us that he sweats freely and that we would need to break from filming every few minutes so that the make-up girl – who we would provide incidentally – could powder his brow.

Odd, then, that the venue for this interview should be a non-air-conditioned Tex-Mex joint in one of Houston's rougher zones, on one of the hottest evenings of the year. It was 114 degrees outside, and about twice that under our lights. Dusty had a big problem.

We tried tightening the shot on Frank and Billy while the make-up girl mopped Dusty down, but by the time we'd swung round to film his answer to a particular question it was Niagara time all over again.

Then someone produced a hand-held Pifco fan and suggested Dusty used it to stay cool until the camera was on him. Then he could lower it, answer the question, and all would be well. Great idea. Dusty liked it too, and even Murray, our sound man, said its gentle hum was no big deal.

I was busy talking to Billy when the inevitable happened. The fan somehow wound up in the beard and it took an hour to get it out again.

This was a testing point. If these guys were arsehole rock stars, they'd be out of the place like a shot. But they stayed. Billy couldn't do much else. He was laughing the laugh of someone who was about to burst.

They are car nuts. In their early days, they found a big, wire-mesh ball with a seat inside. God knows what it had been built for originally but they invented a game where someone would climb inside, shut the mesh door and then be pushed off the back of a speeding truck.

After Frank survived an 80-mph roll-off, they wrote the song 'Master of Sparks'.

Today, their interest in cars is diverse. Frank has a collection of Ferraris, including a 250 GTO which he's turned into a convertible.

Dusty has a big, fat, chopped 1950s cruiser.

It's Billy's collection everyone knows best. Every day, he uses an old Mercedes SL but he owns the Eliminator, the red hot-rod from those astonishing videos.

At nine o'clock the interview finished, and then the acid test began. A year earlier, after talking to Bob Seger, he'd joined us for dinner, so what would ZZ Top do?

Dusty was out of there but Billy and Frank hung around telling tales and bumming fags. They may be the rock star's ultimate rock stars but they're OK. Ordinary. Funny. They particularly liked it when we asked if they'd written 'Sharp Dressed Man' after seeing our sound man somewhere. Murray has a habit of tucking his shirt into his underpants.

Murray felt right at home at a Texas race meeting. All motorsport fans have no idea how to dress properly but you should see the lengths they go to to look daft in Texas.

The cars aren't much better, because they aren't cars at all. Inevitably, they're pickup trucks, and what you do is line up in front of a big puddle. The lights go green and you try to get to the other side, 200 yards away, as fast as possible.

Some of the modified trucks were quite impressive, spewing up plumes of mud in their wakes, but most people were using stock Toyotas or Fords and honestly, basket-weaving would make a better spectator sport.

Then I found out why the grandstands were full.

The Big Foot truck is an awe-inspiring machine. It weighs five tons and sits on tyres which are six feet tall. To get into the plastic pickup truck body, you climb through the chassis and emerge through a hole in the Perspex floor.

Inside, there's a racing seat, a five-point harness and a dash straight out of *Thunderbirds*.

You turn on all the pumps and hit a big red button which fires up the 9700cc V8. One blip of the throttle to get it running evenly and a gallon of fuel is gone. Think, Wow, this is loud, and another gallon has been spurted through the injectors. On the move, it uses one gallon of alcohol to do 300 yards.

They'd told me that it had an automatic gearbox but that I'd have to shift the cogs manually by pulling the lever backwards. The trouble is, they said 'pull' and not 'wrench'.

At 6000 rpm I tugged on the lever and nothing happened. The revs continued to climb up past 7000, then 8000, until in desperation, I nearly yanked the lever out of its socket. It worked. I had second and we were going ballistic.

This monster accelerates from 0 to 60 in less than five seconds which is enough, but what truly surprised me was how those big fat tyres gripped on the wet grass.

A little flick on the tiny racing wheel and I was hurled sideways as the car canted over and simply changed direction. What made it all especially bizarre is that you could see the action through the Perspex floor.

They didn't let me turn on the rear-wheel steering because they said it makes the truck a bit of a handful. And, I discovered later, they were beginning to wish they'd never let me go out in it at all.

Even after ten minutes, I was still having trouble with the gearbox and the telltale rev counter was stuck at 9200 rpm. This had, apparently, been accompanied by some spectacular backfiring, which had had the crowd on their feet and the owners on their knees.

I was blissfully unaware of the drama and having practised leaping some hay bales, was lining up for a real run, which involved leaping over a line of six cars.

It cut out. What I hadn't realised is that to ensure the crowd would be safe if the driver had a fit, the owners have a remote control shut-down facility, which they'd operated. As I climbed out, one called me a crazy son-of-a-bitch.

Which, from a Texan, was quite a compliment. I've

driven all manner of fast, large and expensive cars but my absolute favourite is that Big Foot. In an interesting country, it would stand out. In Texas, it was breathtaking.

Monaco

Hunting is one of the very few controversial issues on which I have two opinions. On the one hand, I can see it keeps Britain in touch with its glorious past. What sight stirs the loins quite so vigorously as a bunch of hoorays in tight trouserwear coming at you through the mist on a winter morning?

And let's face it, the only reason every fox in the land hasn't been shot, gassed and mangled already is because they're needed for hunting purposes. So, if you like those cheeky little ears and that big bushy tail, you'd better get down to the meet on Boxing Day to cheer the chaps on. These people will hunt come what may, and isn't it better they choose to go after foxes rather than cows or your hamster?

On the other hand, fox-hunting is a barbaric sport which has been taken over these days by ghastly people from neo-Georgian houses in Surrey. What's the big deal about being 'blooded' anyway, a ceremony that should have died when we stopped burning witches. And poor little foxy-woxy being torn apart by those snarling dogs. I'm going to get a Parka and get out there in the woods with my aerosol.

I have the same problem with Monaco. There are two arguments and I subscribe to both of them.

On the one hand, it's a lavatory and someone should pull the chain. It's a police state, where pickpockets are shot but fraudsters are welcome to tea and buns at the palace. Plus it rains all the bloody time.

On the other hand, Monaco is the epicentre of jet-setdom, a playground where you need feel no guilt if you have a hundred mill in the bank because everyone else has more. Plus, it's a sun-kissed paradise.

First, let's get Monaco sorted out. It was a palace and a few ramshackle cottages right up to the middle of the nineteenth century when the casino was built. But even this exquisite building failed to put the little principality on the map. That didn't happen until 1956 when the dashing Prince married Grace Kelly, a deal that brought big-time American investment and the European jet set. Monaco exploded so that, today, it's a high-rise eyesore, a collection of sixties' tower blocks and ageing face-lifts.

But more than all that, Monaco is a Grand Prix. It is *the* Grand Prix. Back in the twenties, the casino was being hit by the Depression and it was decided to organise a motor race through the streets, quite simply to lure the squillionaires back.

There was something awe-inspiring about the result. Street circuits were not new, but to watch the drivers sliding their cars past lampposts, under the Mediterranean sun and round the harbour was really rather special.

The first race, in 1929, was won by a Francophile Englishman called William Grover-Williams. Later, he was shot by the Germans. Perhaps that's why Damon is so unwilling to overtake Michael Schumacher.

Or maybe he can't. The trouble is that it's pretty bloody hard to overtake anyone there. It was designed for a different time and very different cars so that today's carbon-braked monsters are virtually unpassable.

The teams hate it but all the sponsors treat it as their annual bun fight, rolling up in droves aboard ever-larger yachts. They like to bring along their clients who stay in wondrous, glittering hotels and gorge themselves on food which looks like art.

The drivers don't mind it either, mainly because so many of them live there. On any night of the week in the Stars and Bars you'll find Schumacher, Häkkinen, Coulthard, Rosberg, Berger, Boutsen, Patrese, Moreno – even Colin McRae. Monaco is to motor racing what Hollywood is to the cinema. Only Monaco is weirder.

It's governed by an elected assembly that answers to Prince Rainier, so it's kind of like Britain in this respect, except Mrs Queen doesn't interfere, and Rainier does.

Though it measures just three miles by as little as 300 yards in places, there are several districts, of which Monte Carlo is best known. Monte Carlo is where you'll find the big hotels and the casino. Monte Carlo is the jewel in the crown or, if you like, the carbuncle on the arsehole.

Economically, Monaco is tied to France because they both use the same currency, but all similarities stop there. If something costs £10 in France, it will be £2.5 billion in Monaco. One shop tried to charge me £65 for a child's romper suit. We paid £140 for two small bottles of Heineken in Jimmyz, the nightclub.

Money, in fact, is what makes Monaco tick. The police,

the hospitals, the street lighting and all the other state services are paid for by a company called SBM which owns the four big hotels and the casino. This means that the local residents pay no tax.

Think about that. If Schumacher lived in Germany, 40 per cent of his salary would go to the exchequer. By having a flat in Monaco, he saves more than $7 million a year. That's a lot.

All you need do to get in on the act is prove two things: that you have enough money in the bank to last a lifetime and that you're not French.

Yes, to be born French really is to win second prize in the lottery of life. Your wife will have hairy armpits. You will have to converse in a stupid language, in which a table is somehow female. You will know that you have lost every war in which you've been involved for 900 years. You will be forced to eat horses and you will not be allowed to eliminate your taxes by moving to Monaco.

The population there currently numbers 28,000, of whom 5000 are born-and-bred Monegasques who work in the shops and at the factory which makes, among other things, the door handles for the Toyota Carina. Strangely, these people are not allowed in the casino.

The other 23,000 are made up thus: a bunch of Italian Mafia hit men, a whoop of American super-billionaires, a couple of hundred racing drivers, Boris Becker, some other Germans, a crateload of northerners from Britain and even the odd Australian.

Obviously, the appeal of Monaco for these people is strong. No tax. Everyone else is nouveau riche too. And there's no danger of finding you have French next-door neighbours.

But there is a price to pay, and when it comes to property, it's just preposterous. A three-roomed flat half-way up an ugly tower block costs half a million quid. To rent a five-room penthouse suite could be £20,000 a month.

Mind you, think about it. If you had 20 million in the bank, you'd be getting about a million a year in interest, £400,000 of which would go to the Revenue. Rent of £240,000 a year suddenly doesn't seem so bad, does it?

Unless the income-tax people in your own country manage to prove that you don't really live in Monaco at all, that it's just a postal address.

The rules say you must actually be there for six months and one day in each calendar year but there are ways round this. You simply pay your estate agent to go round to your apartment every day to make a few phone calls. Then, if anyone asks, you can provide an itemised bill showing that you really were in paradise on the days in question.

And what a paradise. If you could be transported to Casino Square right now, whatever time of day or night it is, I guarantee you'd see at least three supercars.

The car sales figures here make for some pretty amazing reading, by which I mean Mercedes outsells Ford. Sure, Renault is at number one in the charts but in 1993, Bugatti outsold Rover. Yes, in Monaco, the £300,000, 200-mph EB110 was more popular than the eminently sensible Metro.

And that was its downfall. You see, in Monaco, it is

not necessary to drive the most expensive car on the market, but to turn up for dinner at the Hôtel de Paris and find someone else is already there with an identical car is a social gaffe second only to vomiting on Princess Caroline.

One car salesman told me that the hardest part of his job was knowing which restaurants and which clubs are favoured by which people.

'I simply couldn't sell someone a red Porsche Turbo if I knew someone else who goes to the same parties already had one. I would suggest he bought a different model, or had a different spoiler fitted, or went for a different colour,' said our man.

This, I think I'm right in saying, does not happen in Rotherham, but that's because to the good people of South Yorkshire, a car is just that. In Monaco, it is the last item of clothing you put on before you go out. Out there, a garage is simply a large wardrobe.

The trouble with Bugatti is that, for a time, it was *the* car to have, but when there were more than a dozen fighting for attention in the main square the impact was lost. You'd have been better off with a TVR Griffith.

I know this because I had one and I was the coolest dude in town. You wanna know what Steph's like in bed? You talk to me. Me and Albert? I call him Al – and I'm the one who laughs when he walks into a nightclub and says, 'Okay girls. Stop your grinning and drop your linen.' He does this a lot, apparently.

My Griffith was by no means the most expensive car in Monaco and, having been driven there from England, it certainly wasn't the cleanest, but no one else had one and that is what counted.

Outside every large hotel, club or restaurant, uniformed doormen would indulge in prolonged bouts of fist fighting to decide who'd get the privilege of parking it. In every traffic jam, girls with impossible hair and comic-book legs would lean in and purr. And once, after I'd given it a full-bore take-off up the hill in first gear, I was stopped by an Italian millionaire in a Ferrari F40 and asked if I'd like to swap.

This really does happen out there. I know of one chap who offered to buy Michael Shoemaker's Bugatti after the two met in a gym, but pulled out when the world champion said it was beneath his dignity to actually deliver the car.

Then there was the Australian who ran into a Lamborghini salesman at the Beach Club and asked simply, 'Are they any good?' Once he'd been assured, by this most unbiased of sources, that they were, he ordered a £165,000 Diablo.

Another guy saw a Lancia Delta Integrale cruise by while having lunch at the Hôtel de Paris and told his sidekick to find the owner and buy it.

To be a car salesman out there, you need to move and shake at the right places. You need the right clothes, the right hair, the right wristwatch and an ability to speak at least five languages. Very few people ever walk into a car showroom when they need a car; they meet you at a party and the deal is done.

But you have to be at the party in the first place.

While I was there, Rinspeed, the Swiss car company,

launched its new supercharged Roadster by parking one outside Jimmyz, the nightclub. People saw it, met the salesman inside and a sale followed.

Well that was the theory, but unfortunately, I pissed on their bonfire by turning up in the Griffith. The Rinspeed may have raised an eyebrow or two but that Griffith lowered everyone's underwear. The aquamarine paint job helped, but the noise usually clinched it so I had to spend all night turning down ever-more ludicrous and tempting cash offers.

It's not mine, I'd wail. We don't care whose it is, we want it and here's a fistful of money, came the reply.

Yes, people do go out at night with 50 grand in their pocket – especially if it's their round. There's one woman who leaves the casino every night of the week with £3-million-worth of jewellery about her person. But even at 4.00 a.m. she knows she is in no danger because in Monaco there is no crime.

By which I mean there is no petty pilfering. Largely this is because people with hundreds of millions of pounds in the bank are not big on mugging or house-breaking. Why go to all the trouble of nicking a car when you can just buy one?

But what about the thousands of visitors who come to Monaco every year? Surely, a few of these ne'er-do-wells in their coaches and their shellsuits are not averse to a bit of robbery?

Perhaps, but Monaco has them covered by 160 security cameras that sweep the streets and a further 1000 or so in garages, hotel lobbies and even the lift in our car park.

That, all on its own, would keep everyone in check, but to make absolutely sure, there is one policeman for every 40 residents in Monaco.

Now these guys learned everything they know from Russia's special forces. There are rules in Monaco and if you don't like them, the policemenists will escort you back to France where you can convalesce.

If you are smartly dressed and driving a Ferrari you have nothing to fear, even if you've just broken the economy of a Third World country. It doesn't matter if, after one phone call, you've destroyed a factory in Tennessee and put 500 people on the dole, you are the sort of person they want in the sunshine state.

But if you are wearing jeans and driving a van, you will be stopped at every road junction. Your papers will be checked over and over again. They will harass you and hassle you, only pausing to salute Gordon Gekko as he slides by in a Roller.

Before we could film anything, we needed heavy-duty government permission and there was no question of trying to get by on a wing and a prayer. We'd set up our camera and one of theirs would see, so that within minutes, Clouseau would be on the scene, wanting to know our mothers' maiden names and whether our next-door neighbours kept budgerigars.

Every night outside our hotel two policemen would blow their whistles interminably, pulling over anyone whose face didn't quite fit. In Monaco, it is against the law to look odd.

Unless you have an electric car. There is no greater

demonstration of this country's immense wealth than the government's current obsession with battery-powered vehicles.

They offer huge discounts to anyone who buys such a car, and are about to provide free charging points around the city, but the total number sold to private individuals so far is . . . nought. In Monaco, people are not interested in saving money.

I spent a few days hanging around with one 28-year-old guy who vehemently denied that he was a playboy, but there was some evidence to suggest he was not being absolutely honest.

First, there was his boat which, at the time, was away in America being equipped with new, more powerful engines. Then there were his cars. He said he didn't have so many these days, only ten, but my, what a collection. There was the Bugatti, of course, the Ferrari, of course, the Porsche 911, of course, the army Jeep and the Lamborghini LM002, which he used as a day-to-day runabout. And why not? I mean, it's ideal in the crowded streets and so easy to park.

He also had a 40-tonne truck which he bought to take his Bugatti to Finland where he set a world record for driving on ice – at 180 mph.

Quite a life, I'm sure you'll agree. But we haven't got to the subject of girls yet. He had bedded every single one of the best-looking women in southern France, and maybe the whole of Europe, now I come to think of it, but said that the best was a Texan, who did amazing things with dogs and video cameras apparently.

However, when I was there he was about to take up

motor racing again so he was giving women a rest. 'Just for today', you understand. Then he wandered off with someone who had a blonde head and some legs, but that was about it.

He was one of the lucky ones though. Because everyone there is so rich, and so handsome, and so chiselled, it is quite normal to have 50 million in the bank, no spots and a Mercedes but to end up on your own every night.

Sit in the Café de Paris and just watch. You will see the same cars going round and round and round for hours, their desperate Latino drivers eyeing up everything with a pulse. It's sad, and horrid.

And it gets worse when the Grand Prix rolls into town. The parties get phonier, the rich get richer and the police plumb new depths on the bolsh-o-meter. And on top of all that, the locals pack up and leave.

Half of me says they do the right thing but as I sat in the Sporting Club, watching Belinda Carlisle strut her ample stuff at the Marlboro party, I began to wonder. I had Chris Rea to my left and Jean Alesi to my right as the roof slid back to reveal a monster fireworks display.

The champagne was Bollinger, the caviar was Russian and the waiters made George Hamilton look ugly. This was weapons-grade conspicuous consumption.

But there was more to come. I ended up on a massive boat in the harbour, cummerbund akimbo, talking to a girl who appeared to be wearing nothing at all. It was warm, the stars were out, the vodka was tinged with a hint of lemongrass and all around, truly beautiful people were having a truly beautiful time.

Monaco has been described as the world's first wildlife reserve for humans but if that's the case, let me tell you that being an exhibit there is industrial-strength fun.

India

This chapter is dedicated to Uday Rao Kavi. A fine man.

Calcutta is a remarkable city, known throughout the sub-continent as a city of thinkers, a place where they prefer to discuss cricket than play it. If you can ignore the soot-blackened brickwork and the completely opaque air, you will marvel at the buildings, built with the vast money brought to Calcutta by the British East India Company.

You will seek out the Fairlawn Hotel where you will tuck into winter-warming soup, roast beef and spotted dick. Outside, you will see people cooking their supper on open fires.

Me, I was more taken with a bright-yellow Lotus Esprit Turbo which had just cruised by.

Calcutta is where they make the Hindustan Ambassador – better known as the 1950s Morris Oxford – and the luxurious Hindustan Contessa, an old Vauxhall. Every single car on the streets is a Hindustan of indeterminate age and condition. Some have brakes. Some have steering. Some have suspension. Some have none of these things and are therefore a bit worrying.

But there, in the middle of it all, was the yellow Lotus. What kind of moron would drive a car like that in a country where driving is not a chore or an art form? In India, driving is something you learn to do badly.

And that leads me neatly on to the Indian driving test.

The examiner finds a quiet piece of road and asks you to demonstrate that you can make the car move and stop. Then he gives you permission to take part in what is by far the most dangerous game on earth: driving on the subcontinent.

Visitors may laugh but what passes as mayhem is, in fact, carnage. Even though there are only 29 million vehicles in India – just four million more than we have in Britain – they manage to kill 164 people every day. By way of comparison, we kill just thirteen.

This means that, every twelve months, 60,000 people die on the Indian roads and if you ask about serious injuries, officialdom just shrugs, a despairing look on its face.

Informed sources reckon that upwards of a quarter of a million people are hospitalised and broken by car crashes every year in India. That's the population of a big British town.

And the statistics keep on coming. In Bombay, a city which has more dollar-millionaires than Los Angeles or New York, every single family has been affected in some way by a car crash. Nationwide, one car in five will, at some stage in its life, be involved in a fatal accident.

We may scoff at the Indian's inability to get from A to B without killing someone but, really, it isn't funny.

And despite what you might think, the driving test is not really to blame because most people don't bother taking it.

What you do if you want a permit is send a few rupees to a driving agency in another state, simply asking for one. And by return of post, you'll get it.

One girl that we spoke to decided to actually take the test and then found herself sharing her exam with six other hopefuls. Everyone else, including the examiner, piled into one car and she was asked to drive her little hatchback on her own. After a couple of hundred yards, the two-car convoy stopped and everyone passed, even though five of them had only been passengers and she'd been on her own.

With this sort of background, you can be assured that almost no one on the street has any form of training. But more worrying still, they don't follow any rules.

The trouble is that if you are stopped by a policeman, which almost never happens, you only need furnish his outstretched paw with the equivalent of £2 and nothing more will be said. The motoring courts in India's cities are as packed as the Yukon.

Take insurance, for example. To drive without it in Europe is a serious offence which will result in a possible jail term. Throughout the Continent, high streets are full of insurance brokers and every newspaper carries advertisements for bargains galore.

But none is quite so cheap as the system in India. You just don't buy it.

But even a complete lack of discipline or training doesn't account for what is a massacre. I mean, there are other countries in the world with a similar background of corruption and bureaucratic inefficiency, and they don't get through 164 people every day.

What sets India apart is religion. Being mindful of Salman Rushdie's fate, and not wanting to criticise

Hinduism, I feel duty-bound to report that it doesn't fit very well with motoring. These are pieces from two different jigsaws.

It seems that Hindus have a fatalistic approach to life, believing that everything has been organised in advance and that there is absolutely nothing they can do to shape their own destiny. Que serà serà and fair enough.

We spoke to one ordinary businessman who was by no means a zealot and he explained, calmly, that he would trust his God more than mechanical safety. Indeed, he told of a time when his brakes had failed just a few miles into a cross-country journey, adding, 'I said a prayer and carried on; 250 km without brakes, but it was OK because it was not my day to die.'

But what about the Indian habit of pulling out to overtake on a blind bend or just before the brow of a hill, something that they all do? 'Well,' said our man, 'if it's your day to die, boom, you go.' And what about the person you hit? 'Well it was obviously his day to go too.'

Coupled to this fatalistic approach is a belief in reincarnation which removes all fear of death. Why worry about it, when you know you'll be back as a bumblebee or a sheep some time later? That's not intended as criticism – it's a fact.

But, unfortunately, the belief that you don't control the car and that if you die, it's no big deal, does create problems. About 164 problems every day actually.

I drove from Bombay to Pune and simply could not believe what my eyes were seeing.

The roadside was littered with broken and smashed

trucks, and I'm not using hyperbole here. When I say littered, I mean, littered. Every few hundred yards, there'd be another gaily painted *circa*-1950s lorry upside down in the ditch.

Every tree along the entire route showed signs of battle damage, of having been in a collision with some kind of motor vehicle.

In one case, the lorry in question was still wrapped round the trunk. The whole passenger side of the cab was gone but mercifully no one had been sitting there at the moment of impact. I know this because the driver told me. He'd been sitting by the wreckage for four days, waiting for help.

'Have you got any food?' I asked. 'Oh yes,' he said. 'I brought plenty for when I crashed.' 'When', you'll note. Not 'if'.

Crashing on this main highway is a certainty, for many reasons.

First, huge potholes big enough to swallow a train, never mind my Mahindra Jeep, are thoughtfully marked out by a ring of boulders of exactly the right size to either break your steering or launch you into the pit.

They use boulders in India to mark out all the hazards. When your truck breaks down in the middle of the road, which it will, the first thing you do is surround it with boulders. The boulder is India's warning triangle though, frankly, it doesn't work.

You come round a corner, see the stranded lorry and you are usually still working out which side to pass when you hit the huge stone. Things get even worse at

night because no self-respecting Indian ever uses his lights.
Who needs them when you have divine guidance.

You drive along blind and if, by some miracle, you see
the lorry-sized obstacle, you daren't ease on to the wrong
side of the road to pass because there's no way of knowing if
anything's there. You'll still be braking hard, and deciding
what to do, when the boulder breaks your steering joints.

There are cows, too. Elsewhere in the democratic
world, farmyard animals graze in fields, prevented from
getting on to the roads with fences which are often elec-
trified. But not in India. Cows there have obviously
developed a fondness for small pieces of gravel because
round every bend, your way will be blocked with a
quarter-ton of meat, muscle and horn. One day, cows will
learn to surround themselves with boulders, but it hasn't
happened yet.

Children are equally daft. There are no pelican crossings
with handy beepers for the deaf, no purpose-built speed
bumps near the school. And no Green Cross Code either.
When a child wants to get from one side of the road to
the other, he simply does it, without warning.

There are no speed limits in India but I was so wary of
all the various hazards that I tended to drive around at a
pace which was measurable in yards per year. You would
have needed a theodolite and three satellites to ascertain
that I was making any progress at all sometimes.

I was a glacier with wheels and this was only partly to
do with the ever-present risk of mad children, madder
cows and the boulders. It was mostly to do with my Jeep.

This may have been based on the American beach-party

special but it's Indian-made and Indian-developed. Were it not for the Russian version I drove in Vietnam, I'd have to say it was the worst car in the world.

The only smooth things about it were the tyres. Its steering was supertanker precise and heavier than a photocopier. It braked like a rhino, sounded like a bulldozer in an aviary and nothing electrical worked . . . except the horn.

This, said my guide, Hormazd, was a good thing because in India the horn is 'your air bag, your side-impact bars, your safety belt and your anti-lock brakes, all rolled into one little button. You'd better use it liberally.'

He also told me that for sheer lunacy, Indian driving takes the cake and that if I tried to drive like I did in Britain, I wouldn't really get anywhere.

Well hey, I wasn't driving like I do in Britain, and I still wasn't really getting anywhere.

Continental drift was faster than me that day. And so were the buses. But when they came up behind, they didn't sit there, waiting for a gap in the traffic; they simply pulled onto the wrong side of the road and went for it, irrespective of what was coming.

It didn't matter if we were 50 yards from a blind bend, or just about to crest a hill, or even if there was a car quite obviously coming the other way; they just went right ahead and tried to overtake.

And that's not the end of the story because if, while the bus was halfway past, a lorry wanted to overtake him, he did so, turning a two-lane road into a three-lane one-way system.

So what if a bus was trying to pass and found itself on a collision course with something coming the other way? Who gives way?

'Simple,' says Hormazd. 'Whoever is smaller. In India, might is right. You only give way to vehicles that are bigger than yours.'

So, if while overtaking, the bus finds itself head to head with a car, the car driver heads for the ditch. If, on the other hand, it's a big truck, the bus will swerve back onto his side of the road . . . where I was.

Of course, if the bus had found itself heading for another bus of an identical size and weight, you'd have read about the accident on page 17 in the *Daily Telegraph* the next day.

Things were pretty bad just on the flat coastal plain, but as the road started to get all mountainous it became stupid. It was taking minutes for a bus to crawl past us, during which time we'd gone through six or maybe seven hairpin bends.

Little wonder, at the road's highest point, you slow down to throw money into a small temple, giving thanks for your safe passage so far. I gave the guys there my Amex card and turned for home. I'd seen enough.

But in town, there was more. On the basis that 'might is right', lorries are at the top of the tree, followed by buses, then vans, cows, cars and, right at the bottom, autorickshaws.

Used primarily as taxis, these three-seater subcontinental Robin Reliants are pretty much invisible to all other road users. Crush someone's goat and the villagers will lynch you. Destroy an auto-rickshaw and nobody seems to notice.

I know this because I drove one. I was on a main road, seeing if it really was true that it could do 40 mph, when a car just pulled out of a side turning in front of me. Luckily, I was able to stop, but the truck behind just kept on coming. He didn't brake, he didn't attempt to swerve and he was going to flatten me unless I got going again right away.

If other road users don't get you in a rickshaw, the potholes will. If you don't see them coming, the first indication that you've been over a bump comes when your spine snaps.

But even if you can avoid all the other traffic and the potholes, there's another nasty in store. Cancer.

All of India's cities are polluted but Calcutta has to be seen to be believed – not that you can see it. A spokesman for the World Health Organisation said they'd stopped listing cities in order of environmental risk because the press just latched on to one place, labelling it as the dirtiest place on earth and ignoring the fact that a hundred other places were very nearly as bad.

But he did say, unofficially, that Calcutta is in a league of its own.

Officially, the real reason for the all-pervading smoke is that everyone cooks on open fires, but that's nonsense. The fault lies fairly and squarely with the diesel engine.

It's an inefficient fuel at the best of times, smoky and carcinogenic, but mix it with badly maintained motors and you simply would not believe the result. Every car in

Calcutta is a Hindustan and every one belches a poisonous cocktail which has blackened the buildings and reduced visibility to just a hundred yards or so. The visibility at midday was exactly the same as it was at midnight.

I was there three days and it was like the hayfever attack from hell. My eyes streamed, my nose ran and it tasted like I'd been sucking boiled sweets made from crude oil.

Calcutta had two other drawbacks, too. First, every single patch of green was covered with cricketers 24 hours a day.

And second, the producer stepped in some human excrement which someone had left on the pavement, and it splashed all over his jeans. That was bad enough but the hotel laundry then ironed creases in them, rendering them useless.

Calcutta is shit.

Madras is not.

It was in Madras that I took part in the Blind Man's Rally, a charity do where able-sighted drivers chauffeur blind navigators on a day-long treasure hunt.

The car was an awful Maruti Jeep, I had never been to Madras before and my navigator had the worst BO in the history of the world. Things were bad and they got worse when I saw the instructions.

They were in Braille, which my instructor could read, but the Braille was in English, which he could not understand.

So, at every junction, he would spell out, letter by letter, what it said. Or rather, what he thought it said. His fingers would dart over the paper and then he'd look up with a pleased smile on his face and say, 'Y–J–R–R–U–V.' Well I know I didn't go to university but I'm pretty damn sure that is not a word. And nor was I–I–J–V–V–K–O–Y–Y. And nor, indeed, were any subsequent attempts.

We were helped by the man's astonishing knowledge of Madras which meant that, at any given point, he knew exactly where we were. But at the same time, we were hindered hugely by the fact that neither of us knew where we were supposed to be.

Madras is not an especially big city but by some miracle, we managed to miss every single one of the fifteen check-points. We also lost the crew, who were supposed to be filming our attempts. And we were so late back, dinner was finished.

But that said, when I'm on my deathbed and someone asks me which day I would most like to relive, it would be that one. I laughed more at that endless stream of letters than I did when I once saw Lord Longford fall over.

This is the point with India. If you can ignore the very obvious poverty, the leprosy and their staggering inability to drive motor vehicles, it is a funny place.

And we have America to thank for that. Whereas the superpower's tentacles have infiltrated pretty well every other country on earth to the point that, even in Peking, people know of Bruce Springsteen, India is clean.

You can buy a Big Mac in Reykjavik and listen to Austra-lian disc jockeys talking about what's coming up 'this hour'.

But in India, I could find nothing that would remind Wilbur or Myrtle of home. India is a larger, hotter version of Britain *circa* 1950.

They have inherited our love affair with bureaucracy, our legal system and, best of all, our figures of speech from a bygone age.

When driving past the railway station in Bombay – a building the Americans would call impressive, or cool – I asked my taxi driver what it was. 'From British days,' he said. 'Most odd and solid.'

Later, another taxi driver described the mosque in the middle of the bay as 'most sturdy and spiffing'. This was fantastic.

But it paled into insignificance alongside the message you find on the label of a bottle of Kingfisher beer. It says 'most thrilling chilled'. Isn't that just wonderful?

The Americanisation of the English language just hasn't happened on the subcontinent so that when you pick up a newspaper there, it appears to have been written by Mr Grayson and Mr Cholmondley-Warner.

Just 10 per cent of the nation actually speaks English but it is English, not American, and anyway, 10 per cent of the Indian population equates to very nearly one hundred million people.

And seemingly each one of them queued up each night, in the bars and nightclubs and restaurants to tell us that every educated Indian has a love–hate relationship with the old Motherland. They hate us for having been there but are grateful that it was us, and not the Spaniards or the Germans.

I was told by one, 'The British had a habit of raping a country, of taking what they wanted, but at least they never tried to reshape the people who lived there. They left us alone to get on with life. We like that. And you did give us cricket.'

We gave them more than that. We also gave them the Morris Oxford, which they turned into the Hindustan Ambassador, and more recently, the Rover SD1. It was actually built there to avoid a massive import duty, but even though there were only two other types of car on the market it failed spectacularly.

Like cricket, it was complicated, boring and prone to stopping every time it looked like rain, but worse, it was expensive. To fill it up with petrol, for instance, you'd have needed 2,000 rupees, which is twice what the average Indian earned in a year.

Amazingly though, the Indians still haven't given up with us. Indeed, when a British Airways 747 pulls up to the gate at Bombay airport, the entire ground crew come outside to welcome it.

The trouble is that in the 1930s, a quarter of all Rolls-Royces ended up in India and most were subsequently customised with jewelled headlamps, ivory-plated doors and tigerskin seats. They're still out there too, reminding the people that Britain is a byword for luxury.

That's why, when they were looking for a new car to build, they turned to Rover, who have just sold them all the tools to make the Montego. Today, there are twenty different types of car in India but the turbo diesel Austin will be by far the most expensive at £20,000 a go.

Expensive when you think that you must give way at junctions to vans and buses, but there you go.

On the last night of my stay in India I took a long stroll

down the beach in Bombay and watched the sun slipping into the sewage they call an ocean. I saw kids kicking ponies, women urinating on the sand and people whose begging life had stopped when leprosy took their arms.

I thought about the filth, the squalor, the cricket, the massive inequalities and the blundering bureaucracy. I thought about the carnage on the roads, the filth that is Calcutta and the endless head-wobbling.

I was momentarily distracted when a small gurgle from my nether regions announced that my normally iron constitution was under attack from an ice cube I'd enjoyed earlier, but it soon passed and I was able to resume my mental shenanigans. Why, when everything was wrong with this country, did I like it?

It's taken a year to work it out but here's my answer. I don't know.

Dubai

Mine's been an easy life. At the age of eight my mother thought it would be a good idea to take me on a bus. This turned out to be a bad idea when, in a loud voice, I asked why it kept stopping. She pointed out that other people needed to get on and off but I was still confused. And the confusion turned to horror when I asked whether it would stop at the end of my grandfather's drive, or whether it would go all the way to his front door.

'No,' she said, 'it doesn't even go down Spring Lane. We have to get off at the Ivanhoe and walk.' WALK? What was this new verb? What is the possible point of a bus if you have to do walking? But all was well because my grandfather was waiting at the bus stop in his Bentley.

At around this time, my mother designed Paddington Bear, which provided the funds for my education at Repton School in Derbyshire.

I was able to land a job in journalism on the *Rotherham Advertiser* because grandfather, a doctor, had delivered the editor's baby during an air raid in the war.

And I found myself on *Top Gear* after sitting next to the producer at a party.

And my luck didn't run out on *Motorworld*. It only rained when we specifically wanted it to. People turned up at the appointed hour and said exactly what we had hoped. Machinery never broke down. The camera never jammed.

This, for two years and eleven countries, was the law.

But then we arrived in Dubai and absolutely everything that could go pear-shaped ended up looking like an artichoke.

The customs confiscated bits of vital equipment. Our Range Rover caught fire. And on the last night, the very last night of our two-year world tour, we found ourselves in the middle of a religious festival and that all the bars were forbidden from selling alcohol.

Let's take it step by step. In order to demonstrate how Arabs are now more interested in power than purple-velour headrests, we borrowed an Escort Cosworth which had been tuned to develop 420 horsepower.

You may recall that our interview with the driver was conducted at the roadside. This was because it broke down.

Then the falconers didn't turn up, and when they did, three days late, the hunting vehicles had disappeared. Then the heavens opened and in the next ten days Dubai received more than two years' worth of rain.

There were floods so deep, smaller people needed an aqualung just to go shopping.

We were having to rejig our already vague schedule on an hour-by-hour basis, which would have been hard enough in a media-aware country like America. But in the United Arab Emirates to change a long-standing arrangement is to ensure it won't happen. We know this because even if you don't change anything, it won't happen either.

Take the fun run for an example. This was an event where 750 cars and upwards of 2,000 ex-pats head into the desert in their off-road cars for two days of getting stuck and lost, and then stuck again.

The only way it was possible to demonstrate the enormity of such an event was from the air, which is why we'd hired a helicopter.

This had been organised for weeks. It had the backing of their government. The pilot had been briefed. But air traffic control decided fifteen minutes into the flight that it was a military area and that the chopper should return to base.

That meant we had to spend all day playing catch-up with the rest of the competitors – a problem that was made even harder because we had to lug half a ton of film equipment around.

Just 50 yards into the soft sand and a call for help came over the radio from Keith, the cameraman. His Discovery was stuck up to its axles in powder.

Happily, the producer, Andy, was in a 4.5-litre 24-valve, 6-cylinder Toyota Land Cruiser pickup which looked like shit but which, off-road, was unstoppable. It became known as the Millennium Falcon.

And it pulled the Discovery out. And 20 yards later, it did it again. And then, 250 yards on, it repeated the process once more.

Tactfully, we took Keith on one side and explained that, in order to keep going, he must stick the gearbox in first, in high range and never, ever, ever lift his right foot from the carpet.

Keith, we said, it doesn't matter if the valves begin to bounce through the bonnet, or if you're about to crest a brow which may be the precursor of a sheer drop. No matter what, Keith baby, you must drive everywhere absolutely flat out.

Now this was all right in my Jeep, and the director's Range Rover and the Millennium Falcon because they were empty. But on the first bump taken at speed in the Discovery, £150,000-worth of camera equipment leapt out of the boot, ricocheted off the roof and ended up in the passenger footwell.

In the end, we were actually saved by the rain, which gave the sand a more gluey texture allowing poor old Keith to drive a little more slowly. The downside was simple. All hopes of catching the other cars up were dashed.

But I didn't care because I have decided that driving in the desert is better than sex.

Certainly, it's a damn sight rougher, as you are hurled sometimes three feet out of your seat. This means your right foot leaves the throttle and that, of course, is cata-strophic, because the revs die, the wheels bog down and you are then faced with an hour's digging.

But on the flatter, harder-packed plains, you can get up to 100 mph or more, safe in the knowledge that there is nothing to hit, that you aren't breaking the law and that your exhaust fumes can't even find a flower to throttle.

The desert is a big deal in the UAE.

The fun run happens annually, and is organised by the *Gulf News* newspaper for ex-pats who, very sensibly, would never dream of heading out there alone.

Over the last ten years I've been fortunate to see some truly epic scenery. There are the Sierra Nevada mountains in California, the Yorkshire Dales just near Keld and the wall reefs that surround the Maldives.

But for me, the best views are to be found in a desert, and the best desert of all has its eastern fringes 30 miles from Dubai. They call it the Empty Quarter.

There is no life out there, just millions of tons of sand which have been shaped and crafted by the wind. It's a constantly changing landscape but it is never anything other than extraordinarily beautiful.

Fun too, because most nights teenagers take their tuned four-wheel-drive cars to the wastelands for a bit of dune-bashing.

Every night, hundreds of guys choose a particularly arduous slope and see who can get up it . . . and before the tree-huggers start to whinge, I should explain that after everyone goes home, one breath of wind is all it takes to erase their tracks.

Now I had a 4.6-litre Range Rover which had air suspension and the pressure in its tyres lowered to 10 psi. Here, then, was the world's best off-roader which had been modified to do the job. And it failed.

The reason is simple – 4.6 litres is not enough. You need a lot more than that, and special sand tyres which are nearly slick. Some skill is useful too.

One guy had an ordinary-looking Nissan Patrol and he could dawdle up the slope, changing gear halfway up if he felt like it. He could stop at 45 degrees, and then get going again.

On the rear window there was a large question mark, which provided the perfect answer for anyone wanting to know what sort of engine it had. A big one. With some turbos, at a guess.

We were deeply impressed but there was more to come because these guys like to drive home on two wheels. One veered on to the wrong side of the dual carriageway and then swerved back so that his Nissan hoiked itself over . . . and stayed like that for fifteen miles!

Each to his own. In England, young chaps show off by seeing who can drink the most pints, and who will order the hottest curry. Out there, where they don't drink, the challenge is to see who can drive the furthest at 45 degrees.

Others do doughnuts while some indulge in full-bore, smoking-tyred, wailing-banshee quarter-mile tests.

The police don't really care, and nor do passing motorists, most of whom simply pull on to the hard shoulder for a gawp.

Let's be honest. The average Arab isn't really in a hurry to get anywhere. I mean, it's not like the next meeting will be make or break. And they don't need to get the cheque into the bank on time.

These guys are so rich, it makes your teeth itch. If Elton John lived out there, they'd put him on income support. We worry about winning the lottery when most of the Arabs are getting that sort of cash every day. Some, I suspect, make millions every hour.

It made the news in Britain when a Dubai sheikh wandered into a London furniture store and bought every single item in the showroom. The bill was £325,000 which is nothing. They lose £325,000 down the back of the sofa most nights.

I know of one woman who made a set of curtains for someone's house. He paid the £340 bill . . . and gave her a Jaguar XJS convertible as a present.

When Mohammed Bin Sulayem said on the programme, 'I am not a rich man,' viewers all over Britain gasped because I'd already explained that he had a Ferrari F50, a tuned F40, a Jaguar XJ220 and a Porsche 959. In addition, he has a Bentley Continental R and a Toyota Previa.

Here are some more details. None of them is insured and every night, they sit in his drive with the keys in the ignition. Sure there isn't much crime in the UAE but we're talking here about maybe £2.2-million-worth of cars.

And yet he's right. Comparatively speaking, in Dubai, he's just an average, ordinary Joe.

The Rainbow Sheikh, on the other hand, is not at all average. Even by Sultan of Brunei standards, this guy is a serious player.

We were shown first of all to the garage at one of his homes in Abu Dhabi and I must confess that I was dumbfounded. To my left, I was dimly aware of a biplane and a helicopter and a couple of rather nice gin palaces, but they were bit-part actors in an RSC performance of *Twelfth Night*.

I walked around the white-painted . . . hangar is the only word, taking stock of the machinery. It was so diverse: over there a Mini, and here, a Dodge Viper. There was an amphi car, a Lamborghini LM002, a Citroën 2CV, a wild array of pickup trucks and vans and, over on the left-hand wall, seven S-Class Mercs, each one painted a different colour of the rainbow.

It was the same story on the inside, too. The leather-work and the dash matched the exterior and, when you opened the boot, even the three SLR rifles were colour coordinated.

It turns out that these had been built for the Rainbow Sheikh's wedding, and that Mercedes had stopped their production lines in Germany to paint and trim them specially. He really is an extremely good customer. He even has an SL where the bumpers, door handles and gear lever are gold. And I'm talking real, solid, gold.

What I adored about that collection of cars is that they were not themed and ordered. There was no structure as you would find in a museum. This was one man's collection of cars he simply likes.

Cars he doesn't like, in case you're interested, are given away to the staff.

It took the best part of two hours to tour his garage, and then we were shown into another garage where he keeps his everyday cars.

Here there were maybe 30 or 40 Mercedes G Wagens and Hummers. Let's be conservative and guess at £1.5-million-worth of metal.

I turned to an aide and asked jokingly if the Sheikh had more garages we should see. 'Certainly,' he said, 'but it is a long drive to his other houses.' Jesus Christ.

Having met his metal, it was now time to meet the man – His Highness Sheikh Hamad Bin Hamdan Al Nahyan.

He strode down the steps, resplendent in a dishdash and a silk Savile Row jacket. A titanium Breitling was on his left wrist. He was 35 years old.

His youthfulness was one shock, but the next one sent me reeling. 'It is a great honour to have you here,' he said. 'I have had many television companies at my house but never before has the British Broadcasting Corporation been here. It is the ultimate thing for me.'

Well now, all over the world the BBC is revered like some kind of god and doors that would remain closed to ITV are flung open, but this was something else. Here was a genuine piece of Arab royalty explaining that by far the best programme on his 400-channel TV was *Top Gear*.

We strolled through the grounds and he explained he had just bought an AMG tuned Mercedes C-Class for his son – who is eleven – and that in all his life, he has never sold a car. 'It would not look good. It would not be the done thing, so I give them away.'

Has he ever left one in the desert, when the ashtrays were full, I wondered. 'No,' came the reply. 'But if you know where such a car is, do let me know.'

He then asked why my Range Rover had Kuwaiti plates. And I explained that Land Rover had been unable to source one for us in the UAE, and that we'd had to have it flown down from Kuwait.

I even made him laugh as I explained how I'd had to go to the airport myself and drive the fork-lift truck to get it down from the ramps because the Indian workforce didn't have the right form signed 68 times in triplicate.

When I finished the rather dull story, he clicked his

fingers and told an aide that he was to buy us a new Range Rover that afternoon.

Oh God, no sir, really, please, we've already got one and honestly . . .

I'm damn sure he would have done it but, before he had a chance, the cameraman asked where he could borrow some lights.

The garage was a great deal bigger than we'd expected and the candles we carry were not good enough. Keith explained that we needed two blondes, some redheads and various other bits and bobs, all by eight the following morning.

It was done, and no one ever bothered to explain why the local news station delivered its broadcasts that day in the dark.

On our tour, he also pointed out his jet boat, on to which he is bolting a Citroën people carrier. He has recently acquired an island off Abu Dhabi and needs to get there as comfortably as possible.

He also showed me his workshops where engineers are currently trying to make a skidoo float. He'd seen our Iceland programme and figures you can combine a jet-ski with a snowmobile.

We wandered into another room which was chock-full of discarded quad bikes. 'Do you have children?' he asked.

'Yes, one, but she's only two,' I said.

'Well now listen,' he said conspiratorially. 'When you buy her a quad bike, you must make sure it is the 80cc machine. The 50cc versions are no good at all. They keep tipping over.'

'Right,' I said, knowing that Emily will get no such thing as a quad bike, ever, because they're too damn expensive.

We weren't there though to talk about jet boats, or Mercs or quad bikes. We were there because the Rainbow Sheikh has built a truck, the likes of which the world has never seen.

He says that his favourite vehicle of all time is the 1950s Dodge Power Wagon, a four-wheel-drive pickup truck much favoured by the oil prospectors who made Abu Dhabi the boom town it is today.

And he's built a larger version of it. A much larger version. It's so much larger that inside there are four bedrooms, a sitting room and a bathroom, all of which are cooled by twelve air-conditioning plants.

To get to the 'cab' you climb a spiral staircase where you will find the master bedroom, complete with a view down the bonnet.

At the back, the tailgate can be lowered electrically so that you have a patio, which can be accessed through French windows.

All this is possible because, though it's an exact replica of the real thing, it's 64 times bigger. From ten miles away, the 50-ton monster looks like a normal-sized Dodge that's just ten feet away. Every last detail is correct, even the wipers, which came from an ocean liner, and the headlights which cost £1,000 each. Their beam is so powerful that you can use them to read a book a kilometre away.

He would have made the whole thing bigger still but

was limited by the size of the wheels and tyres, which are the largest ever made. They came from a trailer used to move oil rigs.

No one knows how much it cost to build because no one was counting, but it wasn't 4p.

It was a military-style operation because the larger pieces were fabricated in Abu Dhabi and then shipped out to the desert where the vehicle was assembled. No road in the world could take the finished product because it's tall enough to let a Range Rover pass underneath, and 24 feet wide. It's one hell of a truck.

And it moves. Between the rear axle and the floor, there's a 6-cylinder, 300-horsepower engine, which is capable of shifting the truck short distances. You can even steer it. And yes, the brakes work too. When I said exact replica, I meant it.

This may be the Sheikh's most ambitious project but it's by no means the first. His first caravan was big enough to have garaging for seven cars and his second is a globe that's exactly one million times smaller than the earth.

That said, the door fits easily into Western Australia. Again, there are four bedrooms and a sitting room; only this time, there's a gallery. Hit a button and the top part – from the Arctic Circle upwards – lifts to give a 360° panoramic view of the desert.

He uses these caravans, and his tent – which is so big it has to be transported on a juggernaut – to go on camping holidays with his family and friends.

'We are Bedouin people. We love the desert and we like to go there in the winter when the north wind blows so it's cool. But we like to have the comforts we are used to in the city.'

It's been said that he has too much money but I am delighted to see someone enjoying his wealth, to find someone who doesn't just sit back and get fat. He was, is, a genuinely humble man who wants a Lear jet now.

Me, I want the Victory boat. This to the world of offshore, class-one racing is what Williams is to Grand Prix. Yet they let me drive it. Well, to be exact, they let me drive it once the rain had stopped. No, I couldn't work that one out either.

The last time I went in such a machine there were three seats so I could just tag along, but this time I found, to my horror, there were just two. One for the throttle man and one for the person who would steer – me.

My instructions went like this: when it flips, reach out with your right hand, undo the seat belts with your left and pull yourself out. There's an air hose here in case you are having difficulties and a belt-cutter there. Here's your helmet. Bye.

Er . . . how do I drive it?

But it was too late. My throttle man, Saeed Al Tayer, had hit the starter and the starboard motor was up and running.

Now, at slow speeds – anything up to 60 or so – the boat is at a crazy angle with its nose in the air so that way back down the deck the driver can't see a bloody thing. And there I was trying to steer this £600,000 boat out of a marina where every other boat was worth five times more.

Whoomph, now the port engine was on song too and I could see Saeed, in the neighbouring cockpit, easing the throttles forward.

Attached to my cockpit canopy, taken from an F-16 fighter, was a rear-view mirror and what was going on in our wake can only be described as biblical.

They'd only given us the small propellers but as the engines were now churning out their full 1,800 horse-power, no props at all would still have made a mess.

As it was, our rooster tails were 60 feet high and a hundred yards long. This is not good practice because it means the boat is trimmed badly, but it doesn't half look good for the cameras.

Then there was a god-almighty bang, the boat slowed and I turned, looking worried, to find Saeed grinning. The automatic gearbox had just taken us from second to third and now we were really moving.

By the time we were in fourth, the boat had levelled out nicely so that just the bottom half of the props were in the water and my GPS speedo was giving a crazy read-out. It said we were doing 106 mph.

I was trying to explain to our on-board camera that the deck which joins the two hulls is like a giant aeroplane wing and that it is supposed to keep the boat out of the water to reduce friction, but I was mesmerised by that speedo.

It said 132 mph. On water. With me at the helm.

Saeed was on the wireless. 'Um, Jeremy, can we turn now please?'

'No Saeed, come on, let's see what she'll do.'

'Jeremy turn now, or we'll be in Iranian waters and that's not good.'

So I turned and the thrill put my hair on end. Damon Hill described this boat as being like a 300-mph fork-lift truck but he was talking horse shit. This had won the world championship and as I turned that wheel, I knew why.

You can actually feel the hull gripping the water in exactly the same way that in, say, a Porsche 911, you can feel the tyres hanging on. Turn too tight or too fast and just like a car, the boat will spin, and roll and you will die.

As we came out of the turn and Saeed hit the throttle hard again, I heard the helicopter pilot over my head-phones. 'Er, can you slow down, please? We can't keep up.'

That night, we all went out with the British mechanics from the Victory team, determined to find out about the boat's innermost secrets. Unfortunately, I must have had a bad pint because my recollections of the evening are a trifle hazy. People think you can't drink in the UAE, but you can. Unfortunately.

I remember wandering around on a roundabout for a while and I vaguely recall being in a bar with some tinsel in my hair but when it comes to remembering how big the V8s were or what effect the hydra-dynamics have, I'm not really your man. Sorry.

The UAE, as I said on the programme, is the world capital of speed, but it's much more besides. It's disorgan-ised like you wouldn't believe. Arabs are more unreliable than a 1972 Allegro. And it was cold too. But when it comes to having fun, nowhere in the world even gets close.

Epilogue: UK

Night after night, stern-faced men and politicians come on the television to tell us that Britain's roads are the modern-day killing fields. Alongside the M4, the Somme looks like a stroll in the park. Severe, blood-red captions flash up, warning us that excessive speed causes 100,000 deaths and serious injuries every year.

The Department of Transport spends millions on gory, X-certificate commercials that tug at our heart strings and lift our right feet. We are shamed and beaten into submission.

But despite what the doom-mongers say, British drivers are the best in the world, by a country mile. We invented queuing and it shows on the roads. We don't lean on the horn every time the lights go red. We don't simply ignore cycles and nor do we dawdle, American-style. We're fast, organised and, despite what the suits say, safe. I'm not playing with statistics when I say that nobody does it better.

And I think it's all thanks to Nissan.

Anyone who is not the slightest bit bothered about cars is likely to be a poor driver. People who don't care about handling or performance; people who buy a car simply as a means of getting about are not going to worry if they indicate left while turning right once in a while.

So what if they trundle along a country road at twenty, causing ten-mile tailbacks? They can't park, don't under-stand roundabouts and are not averse, once in a while, to driving the wrong way down a motorway.

All these people want from a car is reliability. And that leads them, inexorably, to the door of their nearest Nissan showroom.

The good news is that when you or I see a Nissan, we know it may do something unusual and can take appropriate action. By herding all the bad, uninterested, mealy-mouthed and selfish drivers in one type of car, the roads are immeasurably safer.

They're also stationary, which might have something to do with it. Years of under-investment by successive governments mean we have fewer miles of motorway per car than any other noteworthy industrialised power.

I'm always staggered when I consider that we have a fleet of nuclear submarines but no motorways in East Anglia.

We also have no car industry to speak of. Oh sure, we still make cars here but that's because various Secretaries of State have bent over the railings in Westminster and allowed foreign investors to push broom handles up their backsides.

Britain, they crow, is a net exporter of cars but that's only because Honda, Nissan and Toyota set up shop here to exploit plentiful grants and cheap labour.

Blame who you like – Red Robbo, Michael Edwardes, Tony Benn, Mrs Thatcher – but our own car firms are history. Jaguar and Aston Martin are part of Ford. Rover is German and even Rolls-Royce has had to do a deal with BMW to survive.

Great names – like Humber, Singer, Austin, Morris, Alvis, Hillman, Wolsely, Riley and Jensen – are gone.

I wonder, when Lord Stokes went over to Japan after the war to help Datsun set up a car plant, if, for one moment, he could have believed what would happen just 50 years later. The greatest car nation on earth has become a secretary bird, riding around on the back of the German and Japanese rhinos, picking at the fleas. And being cap-doffingly grateful.

There is one area, though, where Britain doesn't just lead the world, we absolutely dominate it. I'm talking about motor racing.

Look at a Formula One grid. Most of the cars are British and among the eight that aren't, you'll find Minardi and Forti, who usually have trouble qualifying.

Even Ferrari, the pride of Italy, realised that if it wanted to get back in the limelight, it needed British help, so their 1996 cars were designed in Woking by a chap called John Barnard.

Benetton is officially Italian these days but does it make or design its cars there? Nope. They come out of a little factory in Oxfordshire. Sauber is Swiss but the engines are British. And where does Mercedes make the power plants that go in the McLaren – Stuttgart? Er, no. Britain.

Then there's the British Touring Car Championship. The Volvos are built in the Cotswolds. The Renaults are from Didcot. The BMWs are from Surrey. Every single foreign manufacturer knows that if it wants to win on the track, it must use British talent.

The Americans know it too. You probably think when you look at the cars lining up for an Indycar race that you are witnessing something completely all-American. You are too, except for one thing. Every single car on the grid and most of the engines were designed and built in Britain.

It isn't exactly a sport but the current World Land Speed record holder is British, as is the faster road car in the world – the McLaren F1. Weird isn't it that the might of Italy and America, and even Japan, is beaten by a tiny British company?

Weirder still is that such a thing can even exist these days. Outside these shores, they think of Fiat or Chrysler as a small car firm but here, we have not only McLaren but Caterham, Westfield, Morgan, TVR, Bristol, AC, Reliant and countless other tiny bits of fiercely independent cottage industry.

Massively expensive legislation and ever more pricey development costs have failed to dent the enthusiasm of these microscopic car firms which, combined, turn out fewer cars in a year than come from Detroit in five minutes.

These cars are for enthusiasts and that's one thing you will find by the bucket-load in Britain.

Nearly every car ever made is eligible for one of the thousands of owners clubs. There's the Bad Car Club, the Club for Unloved Soviet Socialist Rubbish and even ultra specific outfits like the Cortina 1600E register. Got a GT? Well get lost then.

Some say most of the best classic cars ever made are in

Britain, being lovingly nurtured by a nation that perhaps sees cars from yesteryear as a reminder of a once great past.

There are even people out there who collect spark plugs. This would not happen in Spain. One chap has created a display of petrol pumps through the ages. There are blokes who spend more on the carpet for their garage than they do on a child's education.

The government taxes us, snarls us up, admonishes us constantly and then taxes us again. In 1994, they raised enough from Britain's car owners to pay for 428 brand new 300-bed hospitals!

The environmentalists harangue us. Right-on commentators refer to motorists as though we're some kind of nasty disease. And morons with multi-coloured hair camp out in trees to prevent a new road from being built.

But when an E-Type Jaguar burbles by, everyone in the country will take a second, sneaky little look. The British don't have blood in their veins. It's four star.

The following pieces accompanied the BBC television series *Extreme Machines*

Fly Down to Reno

The P-51 Mustang was America's answer to the Japanese Zero. Powered by a US-built Rolls-Royce Merlin engine, it delivered 1500 horsepower and a knockout blow to the flying machines of the Pacific Rim.

However, the P-51 in which I flew was churning out 3000 horsepower and could deliver a knockout blow to my central nervous system – which was very nervous indeed.

You see, if a 1940s' car breaks down, and let's face it they do, a lot, you coast to the side of the road and await the AA. But if a 1940s' plane breaks down it doesn't so much as coast but plummet.

And that's a normal plane. But the one in which I went for a ride had been tuned and fettled to turn it from war plane into a 1990s' racer. The cockpit canopy had been lopped off each of the wings to reduce drag, and the engine had been tweaked to the point where it was a bomb. And the clock was ticking.

In the back, it was noisy and hot and as the thermals rose to buffet our undersides, there were moments of queasiness, though thankfully they stopped short of becoming the spectacular outpourings that occurred in the F-15.

There wasn't time to be sick anyhow. You see, an F-15

struts its stuff in the stratosphere, but the Mustang was designed for low-level performance. So I now know what it's like to do 500 mph 50 feet from the deck.

It's bloody good fun right up to the moment when the pilot decides to turn. This of course means you stay 50 feet up but one of the wings does not. From where I was sitting, it seemed like the tip was actually pruning the bushes.

The pilots need to be familiar with ultra-low flight because in a race they may need to get among the weeds to overtake. But we weren't in a race. So there was no need to be down there so pleeeeease Mr Pilot, can we go back up again. Pretty please? With bows on?

The answer was no, and for an hour we charged about in the undergrowth, flicking left and right to avoid small mounds and molehills.

Death, had it come, would have been mercifully swift and I knew the organisers had a standby act to keep the crowd amused while they hosed me down a drain somewhere.

Last year, after a fatal accident, a wing walker was despatched to keep everyone occupied but that went wrong too. As a finale, the pilot flipped his plane upside down so his wing-walking passenger was dangling underneath. However, he misjudged it a bit and took the guy's head off.

Air racing is under threat in America because its dangerous – and over there, dangerous is a dirtier word than ★★★★.

However, even before the legislators move in, there's a

very real possibility that the supply of old planes will dry up and that will be it.

I'm just glad that I got to have a go before they face the final curtain.

F'in' Fast

I am fat. I smoke two packets of cigarettes a day and exercise is an unfamiliar word. All things considered, I'm not cut out to be a fighter pilot.

Yet there I was in North Carolina, being measured up for a G-suit, ready for a ride in what most experts agree is the world's best fighter plane – the F-15 Strike Eagle.

The F-15 was launched in 1972 and this time the Americans got it right. To date it is the most successful fighter of all time, with a kill rate of 99–nil. A couple have been lost to missiles, but none have ever been lost in air combat. Its nickname is 'The MiG Killer' because most of that score consists of Russian fighters, shot down by F-15-toting Israeli Air Force pilots in the war with Syria, or by US pilots in the Gulf.

Now 25 years old, it can still hold its own against any of the new fighters. Pilots love its huge size and strength, which gives it the ability to carry lots of weapons and fly long range. Its got a gun for dogfights, a massive radar, the most advanced air-to-air missiles in the world and the safety factor of two engines. And tough? One pilot landed safely with a whole wing shot away.

Which I wasn't intending to do. However, all morning there'd been lessons on how to work a parachute, but it's hard to pay attention when you're dangling by your balls from a hook. Then an hour on what to do if the plane caught on fire. I would be connected to the seat by twelve different fasteners, which had to be undone in a certain order.

And finally, there had been some ejector-seat training. If I heard the pilot say 'bail out, bail out, bail out' I was to brace myself and pull a big lever by my thigh, a lever that I was not to touch otherwise. Especially in a high-g manoeuvre when I needed something to hold on to. But would I have to wait for Captain Gris Grimwald to say 'bail out' three times, or could I go after one? Yes I could, but I warned him not to start any commands with the letter B, or he'd be flying solo in a convertible.

My head full of worries and rules, I then went to the simulator for a lesson in how to drop a laser-guided bomb, something we'd be doing on the Kitty Hawk Range.

Then came the bombshell. I was asking how it's possible to study the four TV screens while aligning the crosshairs when I was prone to sickness while map reading in a car.

And Gris said, out of the blue, 'Oh, if you feel sick just fly for a while. It'll concentrate your mind.' And that was it. The next day, I wasn't simply going for a ride in an F-15. Even though I'd never even held the stick in a Cessna before, I was going to fly it.

The acceleration as we tore down the runway was not too far removed from a Ferrari in the initial stages, but when the afterburners kicked in, it was like nothing you could even imagine.

My head was catapulted backwards and no amount of effort could bring it forwards until we'd rolled over and were flying straight and level in formation with our wingman.

But then there was no real sensation of speed, something I said to Gris over the intercom. This was a mistake.

He hit the brakes taking us down to the deck at 150 mph. Then he lit the afterburners and bang! we were nudging the sound barrier. So far so good, but then he put the F-15 at 90 degrees nose high – an absolutely vertical climb.

My trousers exploded as six g came charging into the cockpit on a white stallion. Suddenly, my five-pound video camera weighed 30 lbs. But that wasn't important. Not when I learnt that we'd climbed from 1000 to 18000 ft in eleven seconds. I vomited extravagantly.

And as a present, was given the stick. When Gris was flying the plane was rock steady, but as soon as I was at the controls we began to slide downwards and to the left.

Worried, I yanked the stick to the right, whereupon we tilted and climbed another 1000 feet. Two more moves like that my stomach was searching to expel food I'd eaten on my ninth birthday.

It wasn't until I started to roll it with confidence that fun began to outweigh fear and nausea. In the next fifteen minutes I looped, lit the afterburners and flew in formation with another jet. Well, I thought I was in formation.

I also got to drop my laser-guided bomb . . . eventually. On our first run I looked out of the window for the target. On our second I used the screens but couldn't find it, and on the third I simply released it hoping to line up the crosshairs before it landed.

I fear I didn't just miss the target. I fear I may have missed North Carolina.

But I was past caring. I was also past vomiting. I could think of nothing but going to bed. I cannot begin to explain what 90 minutes in a fast jet does for your constitution save to say that immediately after landing, I fell fast asleep. I also nodded off in the bus taking me back to HQ and again in the debriefing.

But if I ever do take up flying and the instructor asks if I've ever flown anything before, I'll be able to say, 'Yeah, once.'

Clarkson in Drag

Setting up a snowmobile to win a drag race is rather like cooking. You may have all the right ingredients but it's the preparation that matters.

You need, first of all, to assess the quality of the ice and tune your clutch accordingly. Should it come in at 6000 rpm?

Or is there enough grip to permit an introduction at 8000 rpm – the land of maximum torque?

And how many spikes should you fit to the tank track? Too few and they'll break. Too many and you risk the arctic equivalent of wheelspin, and your race will definitely be lost.

Happily, all these details were taken care of before I climbed on board a machine which weighed 190 kg yet was propelled by a 240-bhp, turbocharged V-Max engine. You kneel down, clutching the seat between your legs with your feet braced against the rear suspension. That prevents you from flying off the back when the run starts, and leaves your hands free to counter the inevitable wheelie.

I'd watched as the racers stormed down their 400-metre track in 5 or 6 seconds, accelerating from 0–62 mph in just 1.5 seconds. And I was a little nervous.

But there'd be time for some practise runs before the cameras were turned on. Surely . . .

Er, no. No time at all. So with the light fading, I straddled the machine and attempted to drive through the paddock. The turbo was set for 13 psi and the clutch timed to cut in as the boost began at 6000 rpm. You therefore can't dawdle. This thing is either stationary or off like a greyhound with mustard up its arse.

As I was lining it up on the starting grid, the director said I'd have just five seconds to do a piece to camera during the run. 'And for heaven's sake, don't swear because if you do we won't be able to use anything from it.' Right.

The lights went green, I slammed the thumb throttle open, the automatic clutch cut in with a bang and Lucifer appeared on the horizon, laughing. There was no track-spin whatsoever, despite being on solid ice. The sled simply rocketed off and the skis up front leapt into the air.

I'd been worried about not countering this properly but in fact it was almost natural to keep the taps wide open and simply lean forwards to bring the nose down. Six seconds later, I crossed the line and, for the first time, began to think. Brake at 150 mph and you die. Turn the stubby, shaved, skis and you roll, then die. You sit up on the seat to shave off the speed then v . . . e . . . r . . . y gradually, you apply the brake. And when you're down to walking speed you turn around and head back.

My heart still beating like a washing machine full of wellingtons, we checked the onboard camera to ensure it had been working and found in the course of the run I'd said just two words: 'F★★★ing' and 'Hell'.

100 mph on the Rocks

At the beginning of this epic trek, I made it quite plain that I would climb into absolutely anything, no matter how fast or seemingly dangerous. But I drew the line at white-water rafting.

Odd then that I should be happy to fly halfway round the world on a non-smoking aeroplane to drive up those same rapids . . . at 100 mph . . . in a jet boat.

Mad? Oh sure, but you see, I don't trust anything that doesn't have an engine.

Jet propulsion for boats is now *de rigueur* if you want the finished product to cruise at more than 30 mph. Go to the Isle of Man on a Seacat and it'll be jets that get you there. Go wetbiking off a tropical beach and it'll be jets that provide the thrills. Look at the back of any fast naval ship and it'll be jet propelled, as is Destriero, which ten years ago charged across the Atlantic to take the Blue Riband from Richard Branson.

The idea of jet power was born in New Zealand when Bill Hamilton who, incidentally, was the first man ever to do 100 mph at Brooklands, decided to build a boat to tackle the shallow rivers that crisscross his land.

Jet planes were all the rage so he started work on the same idea, sucking water into an impeller then thrusting it out of the back below the waterline.

It was, however, not until he employed a young engineer called George Davis that it began to work. George designed a system whereby the water flowed in a straight line, and figured out that the water should be thrown out of the back above the waterline.

'It was basically Newton's third law,' he told me. 'If you fire a bullet, the rifle recoils. So we fired the water one way and the boat was pushed the other.' It was simple stuff and what made it better still is that no rudder was needed. To turn the boat you simply turned the jet outlet pipe.

So now they had a boat with no prop and no rudder, a boat that only needed a couple of inches of water. All they needed to do was show the world how clever they'd been.

In the 1950s, Bill's sons Jon and George led an expedition up the Colorado, taking their jet-propelled boats through mountainous rapids and right through the Grand Canyon. It was the first time this had ever been achieved and, thanks to the dams, it'll never be done again.

Having succeeded there, intrepid explorer John Blashford-Snell invited the Kiwis to provide back-up on his Congo expedition and later, Sir Hillary used their jet boats on the Ganges.

The ferocity they faced was simply horrendous; 50-foot-high waves, whirlpools 100 yards across, fallen trees being swept towards them and, on the Congo, seagoing conditions superimposed on violent river water.

The jet boat had proved itself and became a global smash hit. But the story doesn't quite end there. Pop down to a river for a quiet picnic in New Zealand these days and you won't have long to wait before the tranquillity is shattered by a 15-foot jet boat tearing by at upwards of 100 mph.

Powered by big and unsilenced V8s, these aluminium-hulled boats meet at a prearranged point and simply race to another spot which may well be 100 miles away.

There's no point learning the river either, because one storm can completely change everything. You just boat along hoping that the motor keeps going because without it there is no steering. And you will crash.

I went for a ride and was amazed. In an ordinary boat, you're constantly looking for signs of deep water to keep the prop safe but in a jet boat you can run quite happily with the hull very obviously on the bottom – and it doesn't matter.

Water that wouldn't even dampen a pair of ballet shoes is deep enough for these boys. The trouble is that pic-nickers and Maoris don't take kindly to city boys dancing with the devil in what even I'll admit is spectacular countryside. Which is one of the reasons why the Kiwis have now come up with jet sprinting.

The boats are small – twelve feet long – but the engines are not. Mine had a supercharged V8.

The actual course closely resembles a plate of spaghetti with no straight bits and an endless array of twists, turns and crossovers. Trying to drive the boat and concentrate on which way to go as well would be impossible so you take along a passenger who, using hand signals, keeps you posted.

The water is a couple of feet deep or so, but the drivers cut corners, actually running on the bank for half an hour or so. This however, is not so they can get past the boat in front. I was saddened to learn that the jet boats go out there all alone, racing purely against the clock – until I heard the reason.

This is that the jet units are so powerful that they use all the water in the river. Peer through the spray from that outlet pipe and you'll see that the channel behind the boat is actually bone dry, so if you come up behind another boat, you just . . . stop.

Driving the boat is hard because you must forget everything you ever learned in a car. You lift off in the micro straights so that you can engage full power and thus have full turning ability through the corners.

It sounded all right in theory but from the passenger's seat, I don't ever remember going in a straight line. It was simply a case of turning left, left, left, right, left, right, right . . . that quickly and constantly.

To get a feeling for what it's like you must imagine that God has hold of the back end and is trying to shake your teeth out. At the same time, he is also trying to rip your head off by shaking it from side to side. And all this is going on while you are inside the sound system at a Metallica concert.

Now, you may be wondering why God would want to smash these boats, and I think I have the answer.

He's jealous because man has invented something wonderful – and something He never thought of.

Picture Credits

Italy: Tony Waite; Cuba: Morris Carpenter/Insight; Detroit: Andy Wilman; Iceland: Andy Wilman; Japan: Peto Seaward/Tony Stone Images; Switzerland (2): Morris Carpenter/Insight; Vietnam: Norman Lomax; Australia: Oliver Strewe/Tony Stone Images; Texas: Andy Wilman; Monaco: Andy Wilman; India: Alain Evrard/Robert Harding Picture Library; F-15: copyright © George Hall/CORBIS.

JEREMY CLARKSON

CLARKSON ON CARS

Jeremy Clarkson is the second best motoring writer in Britain. For twenty years he's been driving cars, writing about them and occasionally voicing his opinions on *Top Gear*.

No one on in the business is taller.

Here, he has collected his best car columns and stories in which he waxes lyrical on topics as useful and diverse as:

The perils of bicycle ownership

Why Australians – not Brits – need bull bars

Why soon only geriatrics will be driving BMWs

The difficulty of deciding on the best car for your wedding

Why Jesus's dad would have owned a Nissan Bluebird

… And why it is that bus lanes cause traffic jams

Irreverent, damn funny and offensive to almost everyone, this is writing with its foot to the floor, the brake lines cut and the speed limit smashed to smithereens. Sit back and enjoy the ride.

JEREMY CLARKSON

I KNOW YOU GOT SOUL

Some machines have it and others don't: Soul. They take your breath away, and your heart beats a little faster just knowing that they exist. They may not be the fastest, most efficient, even the best in their class – but they were designed and built by people who loved them, and we can't help but love them back.

For instance,

Zeppelin airships, whilst disastrously explosive in almost every case, were elegant and beautiful bubbles in the air.

The battleships were some of the least effective weapons of war ever built, but made the people who paid for them feel good.

Despite two tragic crashes, the *Space Shuttle* still leaves you with a rocket in your pocket.

Some might dismiss this list as simply being for boys and their toys, but, as Jeremy Clarkson shows, that is to miss the point of what makes the sweep of the Hoover Dam sexier than a supermodel's curves; why the *Princess* flying boat could give white elephants a good name; and why the *Flying Scotsman* beats the Bullet Train every time.

In *I Know You Got Soul*, Jeremy Clarkson celebrates, in his own inimitable style, the machines that matter to us, and tells the stories of the geniuses, boffins and crackpots who put the ghost in the machine.

read more

JEREMY CLARKSON

If you enjoyed this book, there are several ways you can read more by the same author and make sure you get the inside track on all Penguin books.

Order any of the following titles direct:

0141017872	MOTORWORLD	£7.99
0141017880	CLARKSON ON CARS	£7.99
0141017899	THE WORLD ACCORDING TO CLARKSON	£6.99
0141022922	I KNOW YOU GOT SOUL	£7.99

Simply call Penguin c/o Bookpost on **01624 677237** and have your credit/debit card ready. Alternatively e-mail your order to **bookshop@enterprise.net**. Postage and package is free in mainland UK. Overseas customers must add £2 per book. Prices and availability subject to change without notice.

Visit www.penguin.com and find out first about forthcoming titles, read exclusive material and author interviews, and enter exciting competitions. You can also browse through thousands of Penguin books and buy online.

IT'S NEVER BEEN EASIER TO READ MORE WITH PENGUIN

Frustrated by the quality of books available at Exeter station for his journey back to London one day in 1935, Allen Lane decided to do something about it. The Penguin paperback was born that day, and with it first-class writing became available to a mass audience for the very first time. This book is a direct descendant of those original Penguins and Lane's momentous vision. What will you read next?

He just wanted a decent book to read ...

Not too much to ask, is it? It was in 1935 when Allen Lane, Managing Director of Bodley Head Publishers, stood on a platform at Exeter railway station looking for something good to read on his journey back to London. His choice was limited to popular magazines and poor-quality paperbacks – the same choice faced every day by the vast majority of readers, few of whom could afford hardbacks. Lane's disappointment and subsequent anger at the range of books generally available led him to found a company – and change the world.

'We believed in the existence in this country of a vast reading public for intelligent books at a low price, and staked everything on it'
Sir Allen Lane, 1902–1970, founder of Penguin Books

The quality paperback had arrived – and not just in bookshops. Lane was adamant that his Penguins should appear in chain stores and tobacconists, and should cost no more than a packet of cigarettes.

Reading habits (and cigarette prices) have changed since 1935, but Penguin still believes in publishing the best books for everybody to enjoy. We still believe that good design costs no more than bad design, and we still believe that quality books published passionately and responsibly make the world a better place.

So wherever you see the little bird – whether it's on a piece of prize-winning literary fiction or a celebrity autobiography, political tour de force or historical masterpiece, a serial-killer thriller, reference book, world classic or a piece of pure escapism – you can bet that it represents the very best that the genre has to offer.

Whatever you like to read – trust Penguin.

read more
www.penguin.co.uk